Lecture Notes in Computer Science 9823

Commenced Publication in 1973
Founding and Former Series Editors:
Gerhard Goos, Juris Hartmanis, and Jan van Leeuwen

More information about this series at http://www.springer.com/series/7408

Ivica Crnkovic · Elena Troubitsyna (Eds.)

Software Engineering for Resilient Systems

8th International Workshop, SERENE 2016
Gothenburg, Sweden, September 5–6, 2016
Proceedings

Springer

Editors
Ivica Crnkovic
Chalmers University of Technology
Gothenburg
Sweden

Elena Troubitsyna
Abo Akademi University
Turku
Finland

ISSN 0302-9743   ISSN 1611-3349 (electronic)
Lecture Notes in Computer Science
ISBN 978-3-319-45891-5   ISBN 978-3-319-45892-2 (eBook)
DOI 10.1007/978-3-319-45892-2

Library of Congress Control Number: 2016950363

LNCS Sublibrary: SL2 – Programming and Software Engineering

Printed on acid-free paper

This Springer imprint is published by Springer Nature
The registered company is Springer International Publishing AG Switzerland

Preface

This volume contains the proceedings of the 8th International Workshop on Software Engineering for Resilient Systems (SERENE 2016). SERENE 2016 took place in Gothenburg, Sweden on September 5–6, 2016. The SERENE workshop is an annual event, which has been associated with EDCC, the European Dependable Computing Conference, since 2015. The workshop brings together researchers and practitioners working on the various aspects of design, verification, and assessment of resilient systems. In particular it covers the following areas:

- Development of resilient systems;
- Incremental development processes for resilient systems;
- Requirements engineering and re-engineering for resilience;
- Frameworks, patterns, and software architectures for resilience;
- Engineering of self-healing autonomic systems;
- Design of trustworthy and intrusion-safe systems;
- Resilience at run-time (mechanisms, reasoning, and adaptation);
- Resilience and dependability (resilience vs. robustness, dependable vs. adaptive systems);
- Verification, validation, and evaluation of resilience;
- Modelling and model based analysis of resilience properties;
- Formal and semi-formal techniques for verification and validation;
- Experimental evaluations of resilient systems;
- Quantitative approaches to ensuring resilience;
- Resilience prediction;
- Case studies and applications;
- Empirical studies in the domain of resilient systems;
- Methodologies adopted in industrial contexts;
- Cloud computing and resilient service provisioning;
- Resilience for data-driven systems (e.g., big-data-based adaption and resilience);
- Resilient cyber-physical systems and infrastructures;
- Global aspects of resilience engineering: education, training, and cooperation.

The workshop was established by the members of the ERCIM working group SERENE. The group promotes the idea of a resilient-explicit development process. It stresses the importance of extending the traditional software engineering practice with theories and tools supporting modelling and verification of various aspects of resilience. The group is continuously expanding its research interests towards emerging areas such as cloud computing and data-driven and cyber-physical systems. We would like to thank the SERENE working group for their hard work on publicizing the event and contributing to its technical program.

SERENE 2016 attracted 15 submissions, and accepted 10 papers. All papers went through a rigorous review process by the Program Committee members. We would like to thank the Program Committee members and the additional reviewers who actively participated in reviewing and discussing the submissions.

Organization of a workshop is a challenging task that besides building the technical program involves a lot of administrative work. We express our sincere gratitude to the Steering Committee of EDCC for associating SERENE with such a high-quality conference. Moreover, we would like to acknowledge the help of Mirco Franzago from the University of L'Aquila, Italy for setting up and maintaining the SERENE 2016 web page and the administrative and technical personnel of Chalmers University of Technology, Sweden for handling the workshop registration and arrangements.

July 2016   Ivica Crnkovic
                                                                Elena Troubitsyna

Organization

Steering Committee

Didier Buchs   University of Geneva, Switzerland
Henry Muccini   University of L'Aquila, Italy
Patrizio Pelliccione   Chalmers University of Technology and University
          of Gothenburg, Sweden
Alexander Romanovsky   Newcastle University, UK
Elena Troubitsyna   Åbo Akademi University, Finland

Program Chairs

Ivica Crnkovic   Chalmers University of Technology and University
          of Gothenburg, Sweden
Elena Troubitsyna   Åbo Akademi University, Finland

Program Committee

Paris Avgeriou   University of Groningen, The Netherlands
Marco Autili   University of L'Aquila, Italy
Iain Bate   University of York, UK
Didier Buchs   University of Geneva, Switzerland
Barbora Buhnova   Masaryk University, Czech Republic
Tomas Bures   Charles University, Czech Republic
Andrea Ceccarelli   University of Florence, Italy
Vincenzo De Florio   University of Antwerp, Belgium
Nikolaos Georgantas   Inria, France
Anatoliy Gorbenko   KhAI, Ukraine
David De Andres   Universidad Politecnica de Valencia, Spain
Felicita Di   CNR-ISTI, Italy
   Giandomenico
Holger Giese   University of Potsdam, Germany
Nicolas Guelfi   University of Luxembourg, Luxembourg
Alexei Iliasov   Newcastle University, UK
Kaustubh Joshi   At&T, USA
Mohamed Kaaniche   LAAS-CNRS, France
Zsolt Kocsis   IBM, Hungary
Linas Laibinis   Åbo Akademi, Finland
Nuno Laranjeiro   University of Coimbra, Portugal
Istvan Majzik   Budapest University of Technology and Economics,
          Hungary

Paolo Masci	Queen Mary University, UK
Marina Mongiello	Technical University of Bari, Italy
Henry Muccini	University of L'Aquila, Italy
Sadaf Mustafiz	McGill University, Canada
Andras Pataricza	Budapest University of Technology and Economics, Hungary
Patrizio Pelliccione	Chalmers University of Technology and University of Gothenburg, Sweden
Markus Roggenbach	Swansea University, UK
Alexander Romanovsky	Newcastle University, UK
Stefano Russo	University of Naples Federico II, Italy
Peter Schneider-Kamp	University of Southern Denmark, Denmark
Marco Vieira	University of Coimbra, Portugal
Katinka Wolter	Freie Universität Berlin, Germany
Apostolos Zarras	University of Ioannina, Greece

Subreviewers

Alfredo Capozucca	University of Luxembourg
David Lawrence	University of Geneva, Switzerland
Benoit Ries	University of Luxembourg

Contents

Mission-critical Systems

A Framework for Assessing Safety Argumentation Confidence

Rui Wang, Jérémie Guiochet[✉], and Gilles Motet

LAAS-CNRS, Université de Toulouse, CNRS, INSA, UPS, Toulouse, France
{Rui.Wang,Jeremie.Guiochet,Gilles.Motet}@laas.fr

Abstract. Software applications dependability is frequently assessed through degrees of constraints imposed on development activities. The statement of achieving these constraints are documented in safety arguments, often known as safety cases. However, such approach raises several questions. How ensuring that these objectives are actually effective and meet dependability expectations? How these objectives can be adapted or extended to a given development context preserving the expected safety level? In this paper, we investigate these issues and propose a quantitative approach to assess the confidence in assurance case. The features of this work are: (1) fully consistent with the Dempster Shafer theory; (2) considering different types of arguments when aggregating confidence; (3) a complete set of parameters with intuitive interpretations. This paper highlights the contribution of this approach by an experiment application on an extract of the avionics DO-178C standard.

Keywords: Dependability · Confidence assessment · Assurance case · Goal structuring notation · Belief function theory · DO-178C

1 Introduction

Common practices to assess the software system dependability can be classified in three categories [12]: quantitative assessment, prescriptive standards, and rigorous arguments. *Quantitative assessment* of software system dependability (probabilistic approach) has always been controversial due to the difficulty of probability calculation and interpretation [13]. *Prescriptive standard* is a regulation for software systems required by many government institutions. Nevertheless, in these standards, little explanations are given regarding to the justification and rationale of the prescriptive requirements or techniques. Meanwhile, the prescriptive standards limit to great extent the flexibility of system development process and the freedom for adopting alternative approaches to provide safety evidence. *Rigorous argument* might be another approach to deal with the drawbacks of quantitative assessment and prescriptive standard. It is typically presented in an assurance case [12]. This kind of argumentation is often well structured and provides the rationale how a body of evidence supports that a system is acceptably safe in a given operating environment [2]. It consists of

© Springer International Publishing Switzerland 2016
I. Crnkovic and E. Troubitsyna (Eds.): SERENE 2016, LNCS 9823, pp. 3–12, 2016.
DOI: 10.1007/978-3-319-45892-2_1

the safety evidence, objectives to be achieved and safety argument. A graphical argumentation notation, named as Goal Structuring Notation (GSN), has been developed [10] to represent the different elements of an assurance case and their relationships with individual notations. Figure 1 provides an example that will be studied later on. Such graphical assurance case representation can definitely facilitates the reviewing process. However, it is a consensus that safety argument is subjective [11] and uncertainties may exist in safety argument or supporting evidence [9]. Therefore, the actual contribution of safety argument has to be evaluated.

A common solution for assessing the safety argument is to ask an expert to judge whether the argument is strong enough [1]. However, some researchers emphasize the necessity to qualitatively assess the confidence in these arguments and propose to develop a confidence argument in parallel with the safety argument [9]. Besides, various quantitative assessments of confidence in arguments are provided in several works (using the Bayesian Networks [5], the belief function theory [3], or both [8]). In the report [7], authors study 12 approaches for quantitative assessments of confidence in assurance case. They study the flaws and counterarguments for each approaches, and conclude that whereas quantitative approaches for confidence are of high interest, no method is fully applicable. Moreover, these quantitative approaches lack of tractability between assurance case and confidence assessment, or do not provide clear interpretation of confidence calculation parameters.

The preliminary work presented in this paper is a quantitative approach to assess the confidence in a safety argument. Compared to other works, we take into account different types of inference among arguments and integrate them in the calculation. We also provide calculation parameters with intuitive interpretation in terms of confidence in argument, weights or dependencies among arguments. Firstly, we use GSN to model the arguments; then, the confidence of this argumentation is assessed using the belief function theory, also called the Dempster-Shafer theory (D-S theory) [4,15]. Among the uncertainty theories (including probabilistic approaches), we choose the belief function theory, as it is particularly well-adapted to explicitly express uncertainty and calculate human's belief. This paper highlights the contribution of assessing the confidence in safety argument and the interpretation of each measurement, by studying an extract of the DO-178C standard as a fragment of an assurance case.

2   DO-178C Modeling

DO-178C [6] is a guidance for the development of software for airborne systems and equipment. For each Development Assurance Level (from DAL A, the highest, to DAL D, the lowest), it specifies objectives and activities. An extract of objectives and activities demanded by the DO-178C are listed in Table 1. There are 9 objectives. The applicability of each objective depends on the DAL. In Table 1, a black dot means that "the objective should be satisfied with independence", i.e. by an independent team. White dots represent that "the objective

Table 1. Objectives for "verification of verification process" results, extracted from the DO-178C standard [6]

Objective			Activity	Applicability by Software Level				Output		Control Category by Software Level			
		Description	Ref	Ref	A	B	C	D	Data Item	Ref	A	B	C	D
G2	1	Test procedures are correct.	6.4.5.b	6.4.5	●	○	○		Software Verification Results	11.14	②	②	②	
	2	Test results are correct and discrepancies explained.	6.4.5.c	6.4.5	●	○	○		Software Verification Results	11.14	②	②	②	
G3	3	Test coverage of high-level requirements is achieved.	6.4.4.a	6.4.4.1	●	○	○	○	Software Verification Results	11.14	②	②	②	②
	4	Test coverage of low-level requirements is achieved.	6.4.4.b	6.4.4.1	●	○	○		Software Verification Results	11.14	②	②	②	
G4	5	Test coverage of software structure (modified condition/decision coverage) is achieved.	6.4.4.c	6.4.4.2.a 6.4.4.2.b 6.4.4.2.d 6.4.4.3	●				Software Verification Results	11.14	②			
	6	Test coverage of software structure (decision coverage) is achieved.	6.4.4.c	6.4.4.2.a 6.4.4.2.b 6.4.4.2.d 6.4.4.3	●	●			Software Verification Results	11.14	②	②		
	7	Test coverage of software structure (statement coverage) is achieved.	6.4.4.c	6.4.4.2.a 6.4.4.2.b 6.4.4.2.d 6.4.4.3	●	●	○		Software Verification Results	11.14	②	②	②	
	8	Test coverage of software structure (data coupling and control coupling) is achieved.	6.4.4.d	6.4.4.2.c 6.4.4.2.d 6.4.4.3	●	●	○		Software Verification Results	11.14	②	②	②	
	9	Verification of additional code, that cannot be traced to Source Code, is achieved.	6.4.4.c	6.4.4.2.b	●				Software Verification Results	11.14	②			

should be satisfied" (it may be achieved by the development team) and blank ones mean that "the satisfaction of objectives is at applicant's discretion".

This table will serve as a running example for all the paper. The first step is to transfer this table into a GSN assurance case. In order to simplify, we will consider that this table is the only one in the DO-178C to demonstrate the top goal: "Correctness of software is justified". We thus obtain the GSN presented in Fig. 1. S1 represents the strategy to assure the achievement of the goal. With this strategy, G1 can be broken down into sub-claims. Table 1 contains 9 lines relative to 9 objectives. They are automatically translated into 9 *solutions* (Sn1 to Sn9). These objectives can be achieved by three groups of activities: reviews and analyses of test cases, procedures and results (Objectives 1 and 2), requirements-based test coverage analysis (Objectives 3 and 4), and structure coverage analysis (Objectives 5 to 9). Each activity has one main objective, annotated by G2, G3 and G4 in Table 1, which can be broken down into sub-objectives. In Fig. 1, G2, G3 and G4 are the sub goals to achieve G1; meanwhile, they are directly supported by evidence Sn1 to Sn9. As this paper focuses on the confidence assessment approach, the other elements in GSN (such as *context*, *assumption*, etc.) are not studied here, which should be also considered for a complete study.

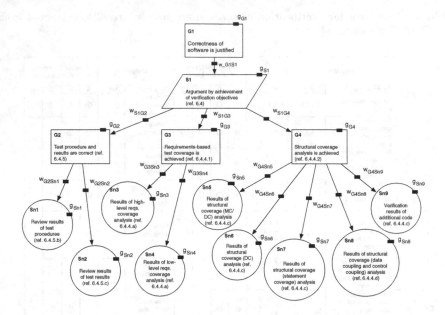

Fig. 1. GSN model of a subset of the DO-178C objectives

3 Confidence Assessment with D-S Theory

3.1 Confidence Definition

We consider two types of confidence parameters in an assurance case, which are similar to those presented in [9] named "appropriateness" and "trustworthiness", or "confidence in inference" and "confidence in argument" in [8]. In both cases, a quantitative value of confidence will lead to manage complexity of assurance cases. Among uncertainty theories (such as probabilistic approaches, possibility theory, fuzzy set, etc.), we avoid to use Bayesian Networks to express this value, as it requires a large number of parameters, or suffers from a difficult interpretation of parameters when using combination rules such as Noisy OR/Noisy AND. We propose to use the D-S theory as it is able to explicitly express uncertainty, imprecision or ignorance, i.e., "we know that we don't know". Besides, it is particularly convenient for intuitive parameter interpretation.

Consider the confidence g_{Snx} in a Solution Snx. Experts might have some doubts about its trustworthiness. For instance, the solution Sn2 "review results of test results" might not be completely trusted due to uncertainties in the quality of the expertise, or the tools used to perform the tests. Let X be a variable taking values in a finite set Ω representing a *frame of discernment*. Ω is composed of all the possible situations of interest. In this paper, the binary frame of discernment is $\Omega_X = \{\bar{X}, X\}$. An opinion about a statement X is assessed with 3 measures coming from DS-Theory: *belief* $(bel(X))$, *disbelief* $(bel(\bar{X}))$, and the *uncertainty*. Compared to probability theory where $P(X) + P(\bar{X}) = 1$, in the D-S theory a third value represents the uncertainty. This leads to $m(X) + m(\bar{X}) + m(\Omega) = 1$ (*belief + disbelief + uncertainty = 1*). In this theory, a mass $m(X)$ reflects the degree of belief committed to the hypothesis that the truth lies in X. Based on D-S theory, we propose the following definitions:

$$\begin{cases} bel(\bar{X}) = m(\bar{X}) = f_X \text{ represents the disbelief} \\ bel(X) = m(X) = g_X \text{ represents the belief} \\ m(\Omega) = 1 - m(X) - m(\bar{X}) = 1 - g_X - f_X \text{ represents the uncertainty} \end{cases} \quad (1)$$

where $g_X, f_X \in [0, 1]$.

3.2 Confidence Aggregation

As introduced in Eq. 1, the mass g_X is assigned for the belief in the statement X. When X is a premise of Y, interpreted as "Y is supported by X" (represented with a black arrow in Fig. 1, from a statement X towards a statement Y), we assigned another mass to this inference which is (note that we use $m(X)$ for $m(X = true)$):

$$m((\bar{X}, \bar{Y}), (X, Y)) = w_{YX} \quad (2)$$

This mass actually represents the "appropriateness" i.e. the belief in the inference "*Y is supported by X*" (i.e. the mass of having Y false when X is false, and Y true when X true). Using the the Dempster combination rule [15], we combine the two masses from Eqs. 1 and 2 to obtain the belief (result is quite obvious but detailed calculation is given in report [16]):

$$bel(Y) = m(Y) = g_X \cdot w_{YX}$$

Nevertheless, in situations with 2 or more premises supporting a goal (e.g. G3 is supported by Sn3 and Sn4), we have to consider the contribution of the combination of the premises. Additionally to the belief in the arguments as introduced in Eq. 1 ($m_1(X) = g_X$ and $m_2(W) = g_W$ where m_1 and m_2 are two independent sources of information), we have to consider a third source of information, m_3 to express that each premise contributes alone to the overall belief of Y, or in combination with the other premises. Let us consider that X and W support the goal Y, and use the notation (W, X, Y) for the vector where the three statements are true, and $(*, X, Y)$ when W might have any value (we do not know its value). We then define the weights:

$$\begin{cases} m_3((\bar{W}, *, \bar{Y}), (W, *, Y)) = w_{YW} \\ m_3(*, \bar{X}, \bar{Y}), (*, X, Y)) = w_{YX} \\ m_3((\bar{W}, \bar{X}, \bar{Y}), (\bar{W}, X, \bar{Y}), (W, \bar{X}, \bar{Y}), (W, X, Y)) = 1 - w_{YW} - w_{YX} = d_Y \end{cases} \quad (3)$$

where $w_{YW}, w_{YX} \in [0, 1]$, and $w_{YW} + w_{YX} \leq 1$.

The variable d_Y actually represents the contribution of the combination (similar to an AND gate) of W and X to the belief in Y. We propose to use this value as the assessment of the dependency between W and X to contribute to belief in Y, that is, the common contribution of W and X on demand to achieve Y. In this paper we will use three values for dependency, $d_Y = 0$ for independent premises, $d_Y = 0.5$ for partial dependency, and $d_Y = 1$ for full dependency. At this step of our study, we did not find a way to extract from expert judgments a continuous value of d. Examples of interpretation of these values are given in next section. We then combine m_1, m_2 and m_3 using the DS rule (complete calculation and cases for other argument types are presented in report [16]):

$$bel(Y) = m(Y) = g_Y = d_Y \cdot g_X \cdot g_W + w_{YX} \cdot g_W + w_{YW} \cdot g_X \qquad (4)$$

Where $g_W, g_X, w_{YX}, w_{YW} \in [0,1]$, $d_Y = 1 - w_{YX} - w_{YW} \in [0,1]$.

When applied to G2, we obtain:

$$g_{G2} = d_{G2} \cdot g_{Sn1} \cdot g_{Sn2} + w_{Sn1} \cdot g_{Sn1} + w_{Sn2} \cdot g_{Sn2} \qquad (5)$$

Furthermore, a general Eq. (6) is obtained for goal Gx supported by n solutions Sni. The deduction process is consistent with D-S Theory and its extension work [14]:

$$g_{Gx} = d_{Gx} \cdot \prod_{i=1}^{n} g_{Sni} + \sum_{i=1}^{n} g_{Sni} \cdot w_{GxSni} \qquad (6)$$

Where $n > 1$, $g_{Sni}, w_{Sni} \in [0,1]$, and $d_{Gx} = 1 - \sum_{i=1}^{n} w_{Sni} \in [0,1]$.

4   DO-178C Confidence Assessment

In the GSN in Fig. 1, black rectangles represent belief in elements (g_{Sni}) and weights on the inferences (w_{GiSni}). The top goal is "Correctness of software is justified" and our objective is to estimate the belief in this statement. The value of dependency between argument (d_{Gi}) are not presented in this figure for readability. In order to perform a first experiment of our approach, we propose to consider the belief in correctness of DAL A software as a reference value 1. We attempt to extract from Table 1, the expert judgment of their belief in an objective to contribute to obtain a certain DAL. Table 1 is then used to calculate the weight (w_{GiSni}), belief in elements (g_{Sni}) and dependency (d_{Gi}).

4.1   Contributing Weight (w_{GiSni})

We propose to specify the contributing weights (w_{YX}), based on an assessment of the effectiveness of a premise X (e_X) to support Y. When several premises support one goal, their dependency (d_Y) is also used together to estimate the contributing weights. Regarding G2, Sn1 and Sn2 are full dependent arguments, as confidence in test results rely on trustworthy test procedures, i.e., $d_{G2} = 1$. d_{G3} for Sn3 and Sn4 is estimated over a first phase to 0.5. For structural coverage analysis (G4), the decision coverage analysis and the MC/DC analysis are extensions to the statement coverage analysis. Their contribution to the correctness of software is cumulative, i.e., $d_{G4} = 0$. Similarly, in order to achieve the top objective (G1), the goals G2, G3 and G4 are independent, i.e., $d_{G1} = 0$.

For each DAL, objectives were defined by safety experts depending on their implicit belief in technique effectiveness. For each objective, a recommended applicability is given by each level (dot or not dot in Table 1), as well as the external implementation by an independent team (black or white dot). Ideally, all possible assurance techniques should be used to obtain a high confidence in the correctness of any avionics software application. However, practically, a cost-benefit consideration should be regarded when recommending activities in a standard. Table 1 brings this consideration out showing that experts considered the effectiveness of a technique, but also its efficiency.

Only one dot is listed in the column of level D: "Test coverage of high-level requirements is achieved". This objective is recommended for all DALs. We infer that, for the given amount of resource consumed, this activity is regarded as the most effective one. Thus, for a given objective, the greater the number of dots is, the higher is the belief of experts. Hence, we propose to measure the effectiveness (e_X) in the following way: each dot is regarded as 1 unit effectiveness; and the effectiveness of an objective is measured by the number of dots listed in the Table 1. Of course, we focus on the dots to conduct an experimental application of our approach, but a next step is to replace them by expert judgment.

Based on rules in the D-S Theory, the sum of dependency and contributing weights is 1. Under this constraint, we deduced the contributing weights of each objective from its normalized effectiveness and the degree of dependency (see Table 2).

Table 2. Confidence assessment for DAL B

	G1								
	G2		G3		G4				
	Sn1	Sn2	Sn3	Sn4	Sn5	Sn6	Sn7	Sn8	Sn9
g_{Sni}	0.8	0.8	0.8	0.8	0	1	1	1	0
e_{Sni}	3	3	4	3	1	2	3	3	1
d_{Gi}	1		0.5		0				
w_{GiSni}	0	0	2/7	1.5/7	1/10	1/10	2/10	3/10	1/10
e_{Gi}	6		7		10				
d_{G1}	0								
w_{G1Gi}	6/23		7/23		10/23				
g_{G1}	0.7339								

Table 3. Overall belief in system correctness

DAL	A	B	C	D
g_{DAL_x}	1	0.7339	0.5948	0.1391

4.2 Confidence in Argument (g_i)

Coming back to Table 1, the black dot, which means the implementation of the activity needs to be deemed by another team, implies higher confidence in achieving the corresponding objective. The activities marked with the white dot are conducted by the same developing team, which give relatively lower confidence in achieving the goal. In order to calculate a reference value of 1 for the DAL A, we specify that we have a full confidence when the activity is implemented by an independent team ($g_{Sni} = 1$), an arbitrary value of 80 % confidence when the activity is done by the same team ($g_{Sni} = 0.8$), and no confidence when the activity is not carried out ($g_{Sni} = 0$, see the g_{Sni} example for DAL B in Table 2).

4.3 Overall Confidence

Following the confidence aggregation formula given in Sect. 3.2, the confidence in claim G1 ("Correctness of software is justified") on DAL B is figured out as g_{G1} in Table 2. Objective 5 and 9 are not required for DAL B. Thus, we remove Sn5 and Sn9, which decrease the confidence in G4.

We perform the assessment for the four DAL levels. The contributing weights and dependency (w_{GiSni}, w_{G1Gi} and d_{Gi}) remain unchanged. The confidence in each solution depend on the verification work done by internal or external team. The different combinations of activities implemented within the development team or by an external team provide different degrees of confidence in software correctness. Table 3 gives the assessment of the confidence deduced from the DO-178C, with a reference value of 1 for DAL A.

Our first important result is that compared to failure rates, such a calculation provides a level of confidence in the correctness of the software. For instance, the significant difference between confidence in C and D, compared to the others differences, clearly makes explicit what is already considered by experts in aeronautics: level A, B and C are obtained through costly verification methods, whereas D may be obtained with lower efforts. Review of test procedures and results (Objectives 1, 2), components testing (Objective 4) and code structural verification (statement coverage, data and control coupling) (Objectives 7, 8) should be applied additionally to achieve the DAL C. The confidence in correctness of software increases from 0.1391 to 0.5948. From DAL C to DAL B, decision coverage (Objective 6) is added to code structural verification and all structural analysis are required to be implemented by an independent team.

5 Conclusion

In this paper, we provide a contribution to the confidence assessment of a safety argument, and as a first experiment we apply it to the DO-178C objectives. Our first results show that this approach is efficient to make explicit confidence assessment. However, several limitations and open issues need to be studied. The estimation of the belief in an objective (g_X), its contribution to a goal (w_{YX}) and the dependency between arguments (d_Y) based on experts opinions is an important issue, and needs to be clearly defined and validated through several experiments. We choose here to reflect what is in the standard considering the black and white dots, but it is surely a debating choice, as experts are required to effectively estimate the confidence in arguments or inferences. This is out of the scope of this paper. The dependency among arguments is also an important concern to make explicit expert judgment on confidence. As a long-term objective, this would provide a technique to facilitate standards adaptation or extensions.

References

1. Ayoub, A., Chang, J., Sokolsky, O., Lee, I.: Assessing the overall sufficiency of safety arguments. In: 21st Safety-Critical Systems Symposium (SSS 2013), pp. 127–144 (2013)
2. Bishop, P., Bloomfield, R.: A methodology for safety case development. In: Red-mill, F., Anderson, T. (eds.) Industrial Perspectives of Safety-critical Systems: Proceedings of the Sixth Safety-critical Systems Symposium, Birmingham 1998, pp. 194–203. Springer, London (1998)
3. Cyra, L., Gorski, J.: Support for argument structures review and assessment. Reliab. Eng. Syst. Safety **96**(1), 26–37 (2011)
4. Dempster, A.P.: New methods for reasoning towards posterior distributions based on sample data. Ann. Math. Stat. **37**, 355–374 (1966)
5. Denney, E., Pai, G., Habli, I.: Towards measurement of confidence in safety cases. In: International Symposium on Empirical Software Engineering and Measurement (ESEM), pp. 380–383. IEEE (2011)
6. DO-178C/ED-12C. Software considerations in airborne systems and equipment certification, RTCA/EUROCAE (2011)
7. Graydon, P.J., Holloway, C.M.: An Investigation of Proposed Techniques for Quantifying Confidence in Assurance Arguments, 13 August 2016. http://ntrs.nasa.gov/archive/nasa/casi.ntrs.nasa.gov/20160006526.pdf
8. Guiochet, J., Do Hoang, Q.A., Kaaniche, M.: A model for safety case confidence assessment. In: Koornneef, F., van Gulijk, V. (eds.) SAFECOMP 2015. LNCS, vol. 9337, pp. 313–327. Springer, Heidelberg (2015). doi:10.1007/978-3-319-24255-2_23
9. Hawkins, R., Kelly, T., Knight, J., Graydon, P.: A new approach to creating clear safety arguments. In: Dale, C., Anderson, T. (eds.) Advances in Systems Safety, pp. 3–23. Springer, London (2011)
10. Kelly, T.: Arguing safety - a systematic approach to safety case management. Ph.D. thesis, Department of Computer Science, University of York (1998)
11. Kelly, T., Weaver, R.: The goal structuring notation-a safety argument notation. In: Proceedings of the Dependable Systems and Networks (DSN) workshop on assurance cases (2004)

12. Knight, J.: Fundamentals of Dependable Computing for Software Engineers. CRC Press, Boca Raton (2012)
13. Ledinot, E., Blanquart, J., Gassino, J., Ricque, B., Baufreton, P., Boulanger, J., Camus, J., Comar, C., Delseny, H., Quéré, P.: Perspectives on probabilistic assessment of systems and software. In: 8th European Congress on Embedded Real Time Software and Systems (ERTS) (2016)
14. Mercier, D., Quost, B., Denœux, T.: Contextual discounting of belief functions. In: Godo, L. (ed.) ECSQARU 2005. LNCS (LNAI), vol. 3571, pp. 552–562. Springer, Heidelberg (2005)
15. Shafer, G.: A Mathematical Theory of Evidence, vol. 1. Princeton University Press, Princeton (1976)
16. Wang, R., Guiochet, J., Motet, G., Schön, W.: D-S theory for argument confidence assessment. In: The 4th International Conference on Belief Functions, BELIEF 2016. Springer, Prague (2016). http://belief.utia.cz

Configurable Fault Trees

Christine Jakobs[(✉)], Peter Tröger, and Matthias Werner

Operating Systems Group, TU Chemnitz, Chemnitz, Germany
{christine.jakobs,peter.troeger}@informatik.tu-chemnitz.de

Abstract. Fault tree analysis, as many other dependability evaluation techniques, relies on given knowledge about the system architecture and its configuration. This works sufficiently for a fixed system setup, but becomes difficult with resilient hardware and software that is supposed to be flexible in its runtime configuration. The resulting uncertainty about the system structure is typically handled by creating multiple dependability models for each of the potential setups.

In this paper, we discuss a formal definition of the configurable fault tree concept. It allows to express configuration-dependent variation points, so that multiple classical fault trees are combined into one representation. Analysis tools and algorithms can include such configuration properties in their cost and probability evaluation. The applicability of the formalism is demonstrated with a complex real-world server system.

Keywords: Fault tree analysis · Reliability modeling · Structure formulas · Configurable · Uncertainty

1 Introduction

Dependability modeling is an established tool in all engineering sciences. It helps to evaluate new and existing systems for their reliability, availability, maintainability, safety and integrity. Both research and industry have proven and established procedures for analyzing such models. Their creation demands a correct and detailed understanding of the (intended) system design.

For modern complex combinations of configurable hardware and software, modeling input is available only late in the development cycle. In the special case of resilient systems, assumptions about the logical system structure may be even invalidated at run-time by reconfiguration activities. The problem can be described as *uncertainty* of information used in the modeling attempt. Such sub-optimal state of knowledge complicates early reliability analysis or renders it even impossible. Uncertainty is increasingly discussed in dependability research publications, especially in the safety analysis community. Different classes of uncertainty can be distinguished [16], but most authors focus on structural or parameter uncertainty, such as missing event dependencies [18] or probabilities.

On special kind of structural uncertainty is the *uncertain system configuration* at run-time. From the known set of potential system configurations, it is unclear which one is used in practice. This problem statement is closely related

© Springer International Publishing Switzerland 2016
I. Crnkovic and E. Troubitsyna (Eds.): SERENE 2016, LNCS 9823, pp. 13–27, 2016.
DOI: 10.1007/978-3-319-45892-2_2

to classical phased mission systems [2] and feature variation problems known from software engineering.

Configuration variations can be easily considered in classical dependability analysis by creating multiple models for the same system. In practice, however, the number of potential configurations seems to grow heavily with the increasing acceptance of modularized hardware and configurable software units. This demands increasing effort in the creation and comparison of all potential system variations. Alternatively, the investigation and certification of products can be restricted to very specific configurations only, which cuts down the amount of functionality being offered.

We propose a third way to tackle this issue, by supporting *configurations as explicit uncertainty* in the model itself. This creates two advantages:

– Instead of creating multiple dependability models per system configuration, there is one model that makes the configuration aspect explicit. This simply avoids redundancy in the modeling process.
– Analytical approaches can vary the uncertain structural aspect to determine optimal configurations with respect to chosen criterias, such as redundancy costs, performance impact or resulting reliability.

The idea itself is generic enough to be applied to different modeling techniques. In this paper, we focus on the extension of (static) fault tree modeling for considering configurations as uncertainty.

This article relies on initial ideas presented by Tröger et al. [23]. In comparison, we present here a complete formal definition with some corrections that resulted from practical experience with the technique. We focus on the structural uncertainty aspect only and omit the fuzzy logic part from the original proposal here.

2   Clarifying Static Fault Trees

Fault trees are an ordered, deductive and graphical top-down method for dependability analysis. Starting from an undesired top event, the failure causes and their interdependencies are examined.

A fault tree consists of logical symbols which either represent basic fault events, structural layering (intermediate events) or interdependencies between root causes (gates). Classical static fault trees only offer gates that work independent of the ordering of basic event occurence. Later extensions added the possibility for sequence-dependent error propagation logic [26].

Beside the commonly understood AND- and OR gates, there are some non-obvious cases in classical fault tree modeling.

One is the XOR-gate that is typically only used with two input elements. Pelletrier and Hartline [19] proposed a more general interpretation we intend to re-use here:

$$P(t) = \sum_{i=1}^{n} \left[P_i(t) \cdot \left[\prod_{\substack{j=1 \\ j \neq i}}^{n} (1 - P_j(t)) \right] \right] \tag{1}$$

The formula for an XOR-gate sums up all variants where one input event is occurring and all the other ones are not. This fits to the linguistic definition of fault trees as model where "exactly one input event occurs" at a time [1].

The second interesting case is the Voting OR-gate, which expresses an error propagation when k-out-of-n input failure events occur. Equations for this gate type often assume equal input event probabilities [14], rely on recursion [17], rely on algorithmic solutions [4] or calculate only approximations [12,13] for the result. We use an adopted version of Heidtmanns work to calculate an exact result with arbitrary input event probabilities:

$$P(k, n) = \sum_{i=k}^{n} (-1)^{i-k} \cdot \binom{i-1}{k-1} \cdot \sum_{I \in N_j} \prod_{i \in I} P_i(t) \tag{2}$$

As usual, if $k = 1$, the Voting OR-gate can be treated as an OR-gate. For $k = n$, the AND-gate formula can be used.

3 Configurable Fault Trees

Configurable fault trees target the problem of modeling architectural variation. It is assumed that the amount of possible system configurations is fixed and that it is only unknown which one is used. A configuration is thereby defined as set of decisions covering each possible architectural variation in the system. Opting for one possible configuration creates a *system instance*, and therefore also a dependability *model instance*. A system may operate in different instances over its complete life-time.

3.1 Variation Points

The configuration-dependent *variation points* are expressed by additional fault tree elements (see Table 1):

A *Basic Event Set (BES)* is a model element summarizing a group of basic events with the same properties. The cardinality is expressed through natural numbers κ and may be explicitly given by the node itself, or implicitly given by a parent RVP element (see below). It can be a single number, list, or range of numbers.

The parent node has to be a gate. The model element helps expressing an architectural variation point, typically when it comes to a choice of spatial redundancy levels. A basic event set node with a fixed κ is equivalent to κ basic event nodes.

Table 1. Additional symbols in configurable fault trees.

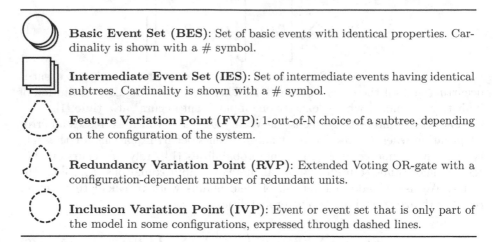

Basic Event Set (BES): Set of basic events with identical properties. Cardinality is shown with a # symbol.

Intermediate Event Set (IES): Set of intermediate events having identical subtrees. Cardinality is shown with a # symbol.

Feature Variation Point (FVP): 1-out-of-N choice of a subtree, depending on the configuration of the system.

Redundancy Variation Point (RVP): Extended Voting OR-gate with a configuration-dependent number of redundant units.

Inclusion Variation Point (IVP): Event or event set that is only part of the model in some configurations, expressed through dashed lines.

An *Intermediate Event Set (IES)* is a model element summarizing a group of intermediate events with the same subtree. When creating instances of the configurable fault tree, the subtree of the intermediate event set is copied, meaning that the replicas of basic events stand for themselves. A typical example would be a complex subsystem being added multiple times, such as a failover cluster node, that has a failure model on its own. An intermediate event set node with a fixed κ is equivalent to κ transfer-in nodes.

A *Feature Variation Point (FVP)* is an expression of architectural variations as choice of a subtree. Each child represents a potential choice in the system configuration, meaning that out of the system parts exactly one is used.

An interesting aspect are event sets as FVP child. Given the folding semantic, one could argue that this violates the intended 1-out-of-N configuration choice of the gate, since an instance may have multiple basic events being added as one child [23]. This argument doesn't hold when considering the resolution time of parent links. The creation of an instance can be seen as recursive replacement activity, were a chosen FVP child becomes the child of a higher-level classical fault tree gate. Since the BES itself is the child node, the whole set of 'unfolded' basic events become child nodes of the classical gate. Given that argument, it is valid to allow event sets as FVP child.

A *Redundancy Variation Point (RVP)* is a model element stating an unknown level of spatial redundancy. As extended Voting OR-gate, it has the number of elements as variable N and a formula that describes the derivation of k from a given N (e.g. $k = N - 2$). All child nodes have to be event sets with unspecified cardinality, since this value is inherited from the configuration choice in the parent RVP element. N can be a single number, list or range of numbers. A RVP with a fixed N is equivalent to a Voting OR-gate. If a transfer-in element is used as child node, the included fault tree is inserted as intermediate event set.

An *Inclusion Variation Point (IVP)* is an event or event set that, depending on the configuration, may or may not be part of the model. In contrast to house events, the failure probability is known and only the occurrence in the instance is in doubt. An IVP is slightly different to the usage of an FVP, since the former allows configurations where none of the childs is a part of the failure model. In this case, the parent gate is (probably recursively) vanished from the model instance.

Classical Voting OR-gates with an IVP child can no longer state an explicit N, since this is defined from the particular configuration. This is the only modification of classical fault tree semantics reasoned by our extension.

3.2   Mathematical Representation

A configuration can be understood as a set of mappings from a variation point node to some specific choice. Depending on the node type, an inclusion variation point can be enabled or disabled, one child has to be selected at a feature variation point, or N and therefore also k is specified for a redundancy variation point.

Event sets, whether BES or IES, are a folded group that translate to single events in one instance. Since there is no difference between an event and an event set with cardinality of one, it is enough to discuss the formal representation of the latter only. The cardinality of event sets is represented through $\#$ in the model, while in the mathematical description κ is used.

The formal representation of classical AND and OR gates needs to include the cardinality κ of a potential BES or IES child:

$$P(t) = \prod_{i=1}^{n} P_i(t)^{\kappa_i}; \kappa_i \in \mathbb{N} \tag{3}$$

$$P(t) = 1 - \prod_{i=1}^{n} [1 - P_i(t)]^{\kappa_i}; \kappa_i \in \mathbb{N} \tag{4}$$

For classical XOR gates, we rely on Eq. 1 as starting point. In addition, the κ value of child nodes also has to be considered:

$$P(t) = \sum_{i=1}^{n} \left[\kappa_i \cdot \left[P_i(t) \cdot \frac{\prod_{l=1}^{n} (1 - P_l(t))^{\kappa_l}}{(1 - P_i(t))} \right] \right]; \tag{5}$$

$$for \ \kappa_i, \ \kappa_l \in \mathbb{N}; \ P_i(t) \neq 1$$

The summation term goes over each gate ($i = 1$ to n) and declares a summation part for the *output* = *true* case in the truth table for this gate. As the child can be a BES with a cardinality greater than one, there would be one summation part for each cardinality, which can be rewritten as κ_i times the *output* = *true* line in the truth table. Also the product part of the formula needs to be exponentiated. All other combinations are eliminated from the calculation.

To make the equation valid for general use in algorithms, the event probability processed at the very moment has to be divided once from the product part of the formula. This makes it unnecessary to clarify which event given what cardinality is processed at the moment. Such an approach is only valid as long as the component probability is smaller than one, which seems to be a reasonable assumption in dependability modeling.

The Voting OR-gate has to be analyzed by calculating all possible failure combinations. With Eq. 2 in mind, a reduced calculation is possible. When using BES nodes as child, the different instances according to the cardinality have to be considered. This is done by defining first a set of sub-sets N_x which represents the combinations of the event indexes and the cardinality indexes. Given that, we redefine the specification of N_j to be the set of all combinations of sub-sets of N_x:

$$P(k,n) = \sum_{i=k}^{m} (-1)^{i-k} \cdot \binom{i-1}{k-1} \cdot \sum_{I \in N_j} \prod_{i \in I} P_i(t) \tag{6}$$

For special cases $k = 1$ or $k = N$, the according equations for OR and AND gates can be used respectively.

The FVP represents a variable point in the calculation that is defined by one sub-equation and the κ value for a given instance. This allows to represent the FVP with a single indexed variable.

The RVP expresses uncertainty about the needed level of redundancy. It is an extended form of the Voting OR-gate. The structural uncertainty is represented by the possibilities for the N value that influence the k-formula. A new variable is therefore defined which gets the different results as a value, so that the impact of the redundancy variation is kept till the end of the analysis. An RVP with a single value for N is a Voting OR-gate.

The IVP states an uncertainty about whether the events or underlying sub-trees will be part of the system or not. It is formally represented by a variable that can either stand for the event probability or the *neutral probability* in case the IVP acts as non-included.

4   Use Case Example

The use case example is a typical high-performance server system available in multiple configurations[1]. The main tree is shown in Fig. 1. Two subtrees are included by the means of standard transfer-in gates. We only show a qualitative fault tree here, but the formula representations can be used to derive quantitative results, too.

It should be noted that intermediate events only serve as high-level description of some event combination, although they map to higher-order configurations in the example case.

The server has a hot swap power supply, so the machine fails if both power supplies are failing at the same time. The cardinality is defined by the BES node itself, so:

---

[1] https://www.thomas-krenn.com/en/wiki/2U_Intel_Dual-CPU_RI2212+_Server.

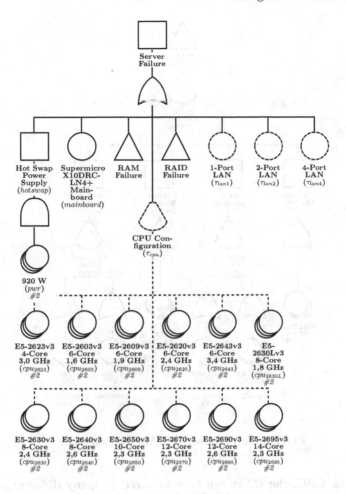

Fig. 1. Main tree for RI2212+ server

$$hotswap = pwr^2 \tag{7}$$

For the CPU variation point, a variable is defined based on the current configuration choice, expressed by the function $ch()$:

$$\tau_{cpu} = \begin{cases} cpu_{2623}, \kappa_{cpu} = 2; \text{ if } ch(\tau_{cpu}) = 1 \\ cpu_{2603}, \kappa_{cpu} = 2; \text{ if } ch(\tau_{cpu}) = 2 \\ \vdots \end{cases} \tag{8}$$

The server can be optionally equipped with additional LAN cards, which is described in a similar way.

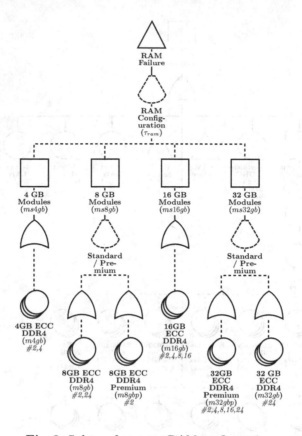

Fig. 2. Subtree for server RAM configurations

As for the CPU, the RAM can be configured in many different ways (see Fig. 2). The failure events for single modules are expressed as event sets with a direct list of cardinalities. This is reflected in the related equation system:

$$\tau_{m4gb} = \begin{cases} m4gb, \kappa_{m4gb} = 2; \text{ if } \mathrm{ch}(\tau_{m4gb}) = 1 \\ m4gb, \kappa_{m4gb} = 4; \text{ if } \mathrm{ch}(\tau_{m4gb}) = 1 \end{cases} \tag{9}$$

$$ms4gb = 1 - (1 - m4gb)^{\kappa_{m4gb}} \tag{10}$$

$$\tau_{m8GB} = \begin{cases} m8gb, \kappa_{m8gb} = 2; \text{ if } \mathrm{ch}(\tau_{m8gb}) = 1 \\ m8gb, \kappa_{m8gb} = 24; \text{ if } \mathrm{ch}(\tau_{m8gb}) = 1 \end{cases} \tag{11}$$

$$\tau_{ms8gb} = \begin{cases} 1 - (1 - m8gb)^{\kappa_{m8gb}}; \\ \text{if } \mathrm{ch}(\tau_{ms8gb}) = 1 \\ 1 - (1 - m8gbp)^{2}; \text{if } \mathrm{ch}(\tau_{ms8gb}) = 2 \end{cases} \tag{12}$$

$$ms8gb = \tau_{ms8gb} \tag{13}$$

. . .

$$\tau_{RAM} = \begin{cases} ms4gb; \text{if } \text{ch}(\tau_{RAM}) = 1 \\ ms8gb; \text{if } \text{ch}(\tau_{RAM}) = 2 \\ ms16gb; \text{if } \text{ch}(\tau_{RAM}) = 3 \\ ms32gb; \text{if } \text{ch}(\tau_{RAM}) = 4 \end{cases} \qquad (14)$$

The RAID subtree (see Fig. 3) in combination with the hard disc subtree (ommitted due to space restrictions) expresses configuration modes of the RAID controller, were each of them relies on some predefined variation for the number of discs.

The determination of τ_{disc} works similarly to the approach shown with τ_{cpu} (see Eq. 8). The more interesting aspect is the representation of the different RAID configurations.

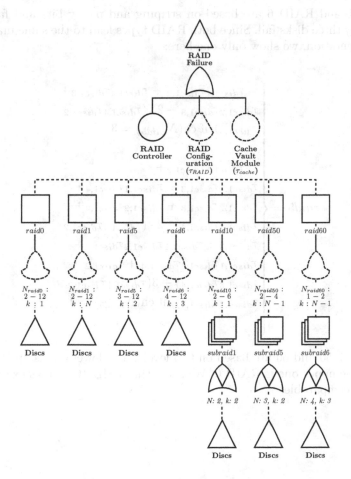

Fig. 3. Sub tree for server RAID configurations.

RAID 0 and RAID 1 are special cases. In the RAID 0 case, the variation point can be interpreted as OR-gate. For RAID 1, the variation point can be interpreted as AND-gate:

$$
raid0 = \begin{cases} [1 - (1 - \tau_{disc})^2]; \text{if } ch(N_{raid0}) = 2 \\ [1 - (1 - \tau_{disc})^3]; \text{if } ch(N_{raid0}) = 3 \\ \vdots \\ [1 - (1 - \tau_{disc})^{12}]; \text{if } ch(N_{raid0}) = 12 \end{cases} \tag{15}
$$

$$
raid1 = \begin{cases} (\tau_{disc})^2; \text{if } ch(N_{raid1}) = 2 \\ (\tau_{disc})^3; \text{if } ch(N_{raid1}) = 3 \\ \vdots \\ (\tau_{disc})^{12}; \text{if } ch(N_{raid1}) = 12 \end{cases} \tag{16}
$$

RAID 5 and RAID 6 are based on striping and parity bits and fail if two respectively three disks fail. Since both RAID types lead to the same mathematical representation, we show only one here:

$$
raid5 = \begin{cases} = \tau_{disc1,1}\tau_{disc1,2} + \tau_{disc1,1}\tau_{disc1,3} + \\ \tau_{disc1,2}\tau_{disc1,3} - 2 \cdot (\tau_{disc1,1}\tau_{disc1,2} \\ \tau_{disc1,3}); \text{if } ch(N_{raid5}) = 3 \\ \\ = \tau_{disc1,1}\tau_{disc1,2} + \\ \tau_{disc1,1}\tau_{disc1,3} + \tau_{disc1,1}\tau_{disc1,4} + \\ \tau_{disc1,2}\tau_{disc1,3} + \tau_{disc1,2}\tau_{disc1,4} + \\ \tau_{disc1,3}\tau_{disc1,4} - 2 \cdot (\tau_{disc1,1}\tau_{disc1,2} \\ \tau_{disc1,3} + \tau_{disc1,1}\tau_{disc1,2}\tau_{disc1,4} + \\ \tau_{disc1,1}\tau_{disc1,3}\tau_{disc1,4} + \tau_{disc1,2} \\ \tau_{disc1,3}\tau_{disc1,4}) + 3(\tau_{disc1,1}\tau_{disc1,2} \\ \tau_{disc1,3}\tau_{disc1,4}); \text{if } ch(N_{raid5}) = 4 \\ \vdots \end{cases} \tag{17}
$$

RAID 10, 50 and 60 are based on two levels. The lower one is an RAID 1, 5 or 6 and the upper one is RAID 0. We show the RAID 10 case as example, the others are comparable:

$$subraid1 = \tau_{disc}^2 \qquad (18)$$

$$raid10 = \begin{cases} [1 - (1 - subraid1)^2]; \\ \text{if } \text{ch}(N_{raid10}) = 2 \\ [1 - (1 - subraid1)^3]; \\ \text{if } \text{ch}(N_{raid10}) = 3 \\ \vdots \end{cases} \qquad (19)$$

The FVP node expresses the single choice for one of the RAID configurations:

$$\tau_{modraid} = \begin{cases} raid0; \text{if } \text{ch}(modraid) = 1 \\ raid1; \text{if } \text{ch}(modraid) = 2 \\ \vdots \\ raid60; \text{if } \text{ch}(modraid) = 7 \end{cases} \qquad (20)$$

The Cache Vault Module can be added to the server to get a battery-backed write cache in the RAID controller. It is represented as IVP. Similar to the voter in a triple modular redundancy setup, it can act both as source of reliability and additional root cause for a system failure. Since the parent node is an OR-gate, the value may become 0, since this is the neutral element for OR-parents:

$$\tau_{cache} = \begin{cases} cache; \text{ if } \text{ch}(cache) = 1 \, (\text{true}) \\ 0; \text{ if } \text{ch}(cache) = 0 \, (\text{false}) \end{cases} \qquad (21)$$

The complete RAID system then ends up being expressible like this:

$$\tau_{RAID} = 1 - [(1 - RAID_{Controller}) \cdot \\ (1 - \tau_{modraid}) \cdot (1 - \tau_{cache})] \qquad (22)$$

At last, the server itself can be evaluated through the OR-gate equation. Combining all sub parts, the overall server structure formula representing the configurable fault tree looks like this:

$$Server \ Failure = 1 - [(1 - hotswap) \cdot (1 - mainboard) \cdot \\ (1 - \tau_{cpu}) \cdot (1 - \tau_{RAM}) \cdot (1 - \tau_{lan1}) \cdot \qquad (23) \\ (1 - \tau_{lan2}) \cdot (1 - \tau_{lan4}) \cdot (1 - \tau_{RAID})]$$

The stated set of expressions represents 4.259.520 possible server configurations, which would otherwise needed to be modeled in single fault trees. Based on the given expression, it would now be interesting to determine configuration-dependent and independent cut sets. Furthermore, each configuration may be related to some costs, f.e. based on the components being involved. The following section discussed some options for such analysis tasks.

5   Analyzing Configurable Fault Trees

Configurable fault trees can obviously be analyzed by enumerating all possible configurations, creating the structure formula for each of them and treating the resulting set as equation system [23]. By iterating over the complete configuration space, best and worst cases can be identified in terms of their variation point settings. Especially if configuration parameters depend on each other, this kind of analysis can be helpful to deduct system design decisions.

Similarly, it is possible to do an exhaustive analysis of cut sets for each of the configurations. This allows to identify configuration-dependent and configuration-independent cuts sets for the given fault tree model as a whole.

An easy addition to the presented concept is a cost function. It may express component or manufacturing costs, energy needed for operating the additional component, repair costs if the component fails, or — in case of the top event — the cost introduced by the occurrence of a failure.

The opposite approach is also possible. Each failure model element can be extended with a performance factor, which should be maximized for the whole system. Adding some system part in a configuration may then decrease the failure probability and decrease the performance at the same time. This again allows automated trade-off investigations for the system represented by the configurable fault tree.

A typical analysis outcome in classical fault trees are importance metrics. They determine basic events that have the largest impact to the failure probability of the system [8, 20]. Classical importance metrics assume a coherent fault tree that is translated to a linear structure formula. In case of configurable fault trees, there are two factors that may have impact: Basic events and configuration changes. One algebraic way for such analysis is the Birnbaum reliability importance measure in its rewritten version for pivotal decomposition [5]. It can determine the importance of a configurable element in the structure formula.

The creation of a combined importance metric for basic events *and* configuration changes raises some challenges. The reason for the non-applicability of classical importance measures here is the discontinuity in an importance function in combination with possibly existing trade-offs between configuration and basic probabilities. The impact of selecting a specific configurations may depend on the probability of basic events. A simple example is a feature variation point that either enables or disables the usage of a Triple Modular Redundancy (TMR) structure. Depending on the failure probability of the voter and the replicated modules, the configuration with TMR might decrease or increase the system failure probability. This leads to an interesting set of new questions:

- Is there a dominating configuration that always provides the best (worst) result for the overall space of basic event probabilities?
- If so, how can it be identified without enumerating the complete space of configurations?
- If not, what are the numerical dependencies between configuration choices, basic event probabilities and the resulting configuration rankings?

- Given that, how is the importance of a particular event related to configuration choices?

The answer to these questions as well as a general importance metric is part of our future work on the topic.

6 Related Work

Ruijters and Stoelinga [21] created an impressive summary of fault tree modeling approaches and their extensions, covering things such as the expression of timing constraints or unknown basic probabilities. Although many different kinds of uncertainty seemed to be discussed for fault trees, we found no consideration of parametric uncertainty.

Bobbio et al. [6] addressed the problem of fault trees for big modern systems. They propose the folding of redundant fault tree parts, but their approach cannot handle true architecture variations. Buchacker [10] uses finite automata at the leaves of the fault tree to model interactions of basic events. The automata can be chosen from a predefined set or custom sub-models. This makes it possible to model basic events affecting each other, but only in one configuration. Kaiser et al. [15] introduced the concept of components in fault trees, by modeling each of them in a separate tree. This supports a modular and scalable system analysis, but does not target the problem of parametric uncertainties.

An interesting attempt for systems with dynamic behavior is given by Walter et al. [25]. The proposed textual notation for varying parts may serve as suitable counterpart for the graphical notation proposed here. In [9], continuous gates are used to model relationships between elements of a fault tree. This is divergent to our uncertainty focus, but the approach might be useful as an extension in future work.

There are several existing approaches for considering uncertainty in importance measures, which "reflect to what degree uncertainty about risk and reliability parameters at the component level influences uncertainty about parameters at the system level" [11].

Walley [24] gives an overview over different uncertainty measures which can be used in expert systems. The presented metrics are based on Bayesian probabilities, coherent lower previsions, belief functions and possibility measures. Borgonovo [7] examined different uncertainty importance measures based on Input-Output correlation or Output variance. Suresh et al. [22] proposed to modify importance measures for the use with fuzzy numbers. Baraldi et al. [3] proposed a component ranking by Birnbaum importance in systems with uncertainty in the failure event probabilities. All these approaches do examine the value of the output uncertainty which respect to the uncertain input values, which relates to parameter, but not parametric uncertainty as in our case.

7 Conclusion and Future Work

We presented an approach for expressing different system configurations directly as part of a fault tree model. The resulting *configurable fault tree* allows the derivation of failure model instances, where each of them describes the dependability of a particular system configuration. Based on clarified semantics for XOR and Voting OR-gates, we have shown how configurable fault trees can be represented both graphically and mathematically.

We offer a web-based tool[2] for evaluating the modeling concept. The underlying open source project[3] is available for public use and further development.

The most relevant next step is the formal definition of analytical metrics that comply with the configuration idea. Unfortunately, dependencies in the configuration space can not yet be expressed explicitly. This flaw already appeared in the presented use case, where certain CPU models are only usable with certain RAM constellations. We can imagine to express such dependencies by abusing house events as 'switches', but it doesn't seem to be appropriate. Instead, we intend to extend the modeling approach in the future for supporting an explicit expression of the relations, either at modeling or analysis time.

References

1. DIN EN 61025:2007 Fehlzustandsbaumanalyse (2007)
2. Band, R.A.L., Andrews, J.D.: Phased mission modelling using fault tree analysis. In: Proceedings of the Institution of Mechanical Engineers (2004)
3. Baraldi, P., Compare, M., Zio, E.: Component ranking by Birnbaum importance in presence of epistemic uncertainty in failure event probabilities. IEEE Trans. Reliab. **62**, 37–48 (2013)
4. Barlow, R.E., Heidtmann, K.D.: Computing k-out-of-n reliability. IEEE Trans. Reliab. **R–33**(4), 322 (1984)
5. Birnbaum, Z.: On the importance of different components in a multicomponent system. Laboratory of Statistical Research, Department of Mathematics, University of Washington, Seattle, Washington (1968). No. 54
6. Bobbio, A., Codetta-Raiteri, D., Pierro, M.D., Franceschinis, G.: Efficient analysis algorithms for parametric fault trees. In: 2005 Workshop on Techniques, Methodologies and Tools for Performance Evaluation of Complex Systems (FIRB-PERF 2005), pp. 91–105 (2005)
7. Borgonovo, E.: Measuring uncertainty importance: investigation and comparison of alternative approaches. Risk Anal. **26**(5), 1349–1361 (2006)
8. van der Borst, M., Schoonakker, H.: An overview of PSA importance measures. Reliab. Eng. Syst. Safety **72**(3), 241–245 (2001)
9. Brissaud, F., Barros, A., Bérenguer, C.: Handling parameter and model uncertainties by continuous gates in fault tree analyses. Proc. Inst. Mech. Eng. Part O J. Risk Reliab. **224**(4), 253–265 (2010)
10. Buchacker, K.: Modeling with extended fault trees. In: Fifth IEEE International Symposium on High Assurance Systems Engineering (HASE 2000), pp. 238–246 (2000)
11. Flage, R., Terje, A., Baraldi, P., Zio, E.: On imprecision in relation to uncertainty importance measures. In: ESREL, pp. 2250–2255 (2011)

---

[2] https://www.fuzzed.org.
[3] https://github.com/troeger/fuzzed.

12. Heidtmann, K.D.: A class of noncoherent systems and their reliability analysis. In: 11th Annual Symposium on Fault Tolerant Computing, pp. 96–98 (1981)
13. Heidtmann, K.D.: Improved method of inclusion-exclusion applied to k-out-of-n systems. IEEE Trans. Reliab. **R–31**(1), 36–40 (1982)
14. Hoang, P., Pham, M.: Optimal designs of $\{k, n-k+1\}$-out-of-n: F systems (subject to 2 failure modes). IEEE Trans. Reliab. **40**(5), 559–562 (1991)
15. Kaiser, B., Liggesmeyer, P., Mäckel, O.: A new component concept for fault trees. In: Proceedings of the 8th Australian Workshop on Safety Critical Systems and Software (SCS 2003), vol. 33, pp. 37–46 (2003)
16. Kennedy, M.C., O'Hagan, A.: Bayesian calibration of computer models. J. R. Stat. Soc. Ser. B (Statistical Methodology) **63**(3), 425–464 (2001)
17. Malinowski, J.: A recursive algorithm evaluating the exact reliability of a circular consecutive k-within-m-out-of-n: F system. Microelectron. Reliab. **36**(10), 1389–1394 (1996)
18. Pedroni, N., Zio, E.: Uncertainty analysis in fault tree models with dependent basic events. Risk Anal. **33**(6), 1146–1173 (2013)
19. Pelletier, F.J., Hartline, A.: Ternary exclusive OR. Logic J. IGPL **16**(1), 75–83 (2008)
20. Rausand, M., Høyland, A.: System Reliability Theory: Models, Statistical Methods and Applications. Wiley-Interscience, Hoboken (2004)
21. Ruijters, E., Stoelinga, M.: Fault tree analysis: a survey of the state-of-the-art in modeling, analysis and tools. Proc. Inst. Mech. Eng. Part O J. Risk Reliab. **224**(4), 253–265 (2010)
22. Suresh, P.V., Babar, A.K., Raj, V.V.: Uncertainty in fault tree analysis: a fuzzy approach. Fuzzy Sets Syst. **83**, 135–141 (1996)
23. Tröger, P., Becker, F., Salfner, F.: Fuzztrees - failure analysis with uncertainties. In: 2013 IEEE 19th Pacific Rim International Symposium on Dependable Computing, pp. 263–272 (2013)
24. Walley, P.: Measures of uncertainty in expert systems. Artif. Intell. **83**(1), 1–58 (1996)
25. Walter, M., Gouberman, A., Riedl, M., Schuster, J., Siegle, M.: Lares — a novel approach for describing system reconfigurability in dependability models of fault-tolerant systems. In: Proceedings of European Safety and Reliability Conference (ESREL 2009) (2009)
26. Xiang, F., Machida, F., Tadano, K., Yanoo, K., Sun, W., Maeno, Y.: A static analysis of dynamic fault trees with priority-and gates. In: 2013 Sixth Latin-American Symposium on in Dependable Computing (LADC), pp. 58–67 (2013)

A Formal Approach to Designing Reliable Advisory Systems

Luke J.W. Martin$^{(\boxtimes)}$ and Alexander Romanovsky

Centre for Software Reliability, School of Computing Science,
Newcastle University, Newcastle-upon-Tyne, UK
{luke.burton,alexander.romanovsky}@ncl.ac.uk

Abstract. This paper proposes a method in which to formally specify the design and reliability criteria of an advisory system for use within mission-critical contexts. This is motivated by increasing demands from industry to employ automated decision-support tools capable of operating as highly reliable applications under strict conditions. The proposed method applies the user requirements and design concept of the advisory system to define an abstract architecture. A Markov reliability model and real-time scheduling model are used to effectively capture the operational constraints of the system and are incorporated to the abstract architectural design to define an architectural model. These constraints describe component relationships, data flow and dependencies and execution deadlines of each component. This model is then expressed and proven using SPARK. It was found that the approach useful in simplifying the design process for reliable advisory systems, as well as effectively providing a good basis of a formal specification.

Keywords: Advisory systems · Artificial intelligence · Formal methods · High-integrity software development · Reliability · Real-Time systems · SPARK

1 Introduction

Advisory systems are a type of knowledge-based system that provides advice to support a human decision-maker in identifying possible solutions to complex problems [1]. Typically, any derived recommendation for a potential solution or description that accurately details a problem and its implications, requires a degree of embedded expert knowledge of a specific domain. Advisory systems are often disregarded as examples of expert systems since there are several distinctive properties and characteristics between the two, despite sharing a similar architectural design [1]. The main difference is that an expert system may exist as an autonomous problem-solving system, which is applied to well-defined problems that requires specific expertise to solve [1]. An advisory system, in contrast, is limited to working in collaboration with a human decision-maker, who assumes final authority in making a decision [3]. Thus, the main objective of an advisory system is to synthesise domain specific knowledge and expertise, in a form that can be readily used to determine a set of realistic solutions to a broad range of problems within the domain area. The user is effectively guided by the system to identify potentially

© Springer International Publishing Switzerland 2016
I. Crnkovic and E. Troubitsyna (Eds.): SERENE 2016, LNCS 9823, pp. 28–42, 2016.
DOI: 10.1007/978-3-319-45892-2_3

appropriate solutions that may maximise the possibility of producing a positive outcome and minimise the degree of risk.

This objective is supported by the basic architecture of advisory systems [1], which compromises of four core components. These are: (1) the knowledge base that lists domain specific knowledge; (2) a data monitoring agent that collects (stream) data; (3) the inference engine that interprets problems from the data and uses expert knowledge to deduce suitable solutions and (4) the user interface for supporting human-computer interactions. In the literature, there are many examples of advisory systems that are deployed in various industrial settings using this architecture, such as finance, medicine and process control [3–10]. However, since system failures in these settings can result in potentially serious consequences, such as loss of revenue, loss of productivity and damage to property, it is important to ensure that advisory systems are both reliable and dependable [13]. In particular, it is imperative to ensure that advisory systems are properly verified and validated, as well as ensuring that the system is appropriately designed for reliability, where it may continue to perform correctly within its operational environment over its lifespan. Currently, there have been many proposals and applications of verification and validation (V&V) tools and techniques that focus on ensuring correctness in the design and implementation of knowledge-based systems [12–16]. It is frequently noted that current approaches in V&V for knowledge-based systems are limited as it is unclear if the system requirements have been adequately met [13]. This is primarily as a result of the presence of requirements that are difficult to formulate precisely, where reliability is considered to be one such requirement.

This paper proposes a formal design method that aims to develop and evaluate a reliable design of an advisory system, which may be used as part of a formal specification. The method simply establishes a general correctness criteria, based on the requirements specification and initial design concept, and develops an abstract architecture that incorporates operational constraints. The purpose of these constraints is to describe the correct operational behaviour of each component within the system, with respect to the correctness criteria, where violations of these suggest conditions for system failures. These constraints are captured through well-established reliability modelling techniques, such as the Markov model, and the likeliness of successful operation under these constraints is examined. The abstract architecture and operational constraints are formally expressed using SPARK. The formal verification and validation tools within the Ada development environment, are useful in proving the operational constraints and thus can be useful in describing how reliability may be achieved in advisory systems.

This paper is structured as follows: Sect. 2 provides a very brief background of advisory systems, in terms of general architecture, real-world applications and current development techniques. Section 3 provides an overview of the proposed design method. Sections 4, 5 and 6 discuss the application of this method to a current advisory system that has designed for use within the railway industry. Respectively, these section discuss: the user requirements and design concept; development of the architectural model and the implementation of this model using SPARK, which is applied to prove the constraints. Section 7 concludes the paper.

2 Background

The basic purpose of an advisory system is to assist the end-user in identifying suitable solutions to complex, unstructured problems [1–10]. In decision-making, an unstructured problem is one that is characterised with contextual uncertainty, where there are no definite processes in place for predictably responding to a problem – that is, well-defined actions that do not necessarily lead to predictable outcomes [2]. As such, problems of this nature require an analysis of all available information in order to properly describe the problem and to attribute suitable and realistic actions that minimises risk and maximises the possibility of yielding a positive outcome [1, 9]. This enables the decision-maker to form an assessment that would lead to a decision. The extent at which risk is minimised and the probability of a positive outcome is increased, determines the overall quality of a decision [4], where a good decision is one that significantly minimises risk and increases the possibility of desirable out-comes.

The architecture of an advisory system, which is illustrated in Fig. 1 is structured according to three fundamental processes [1]: knowledge acquisition; cognition and interface. Knowledge acquisition is the process in which domain knowledge is extracted from experts and domain literature by a knowledge engineer, and is represented in a logical computer-readable format. The knowledge representation scheme used in advisory systems formalises and organises the knowledge so that it can be used to support the type of case-based reasoning implemented in the system. The cognition process encapsulates active data monitoring and problem recognition [4]. Data is processed and analysed to identify problems, based on types of statistical deviations. The cause of the problem can potentially be diagnosed by the system using intelligent machine learning algorithms or solutions to the problem can be identified based on case-based reasoning. The results of this are presented to the user through the interface, which essentially provides various features and facilities to ensure suitable human-computer interactions. This includes formatting the output in a human readable form, explanation facilities to enable transparency in the reasoning process of the system and facilities for user input, such as data or queries.

As previously noted, current literature has many detailed applications for advisory systems in a variety of industrial sectors, including finance, transportation, energy, space exploration, agriculture, healthcare, business management and tourism. From these applications, it is clear that designs of advisory systems are based on the illustrated architecture and perform according to one of two main styles. These are: (1) *monitoring and evaluation* and (2) *diagnosis and recovery* [2–9]. In the monitoring and evaluation style, advisory systems simply monitor data streams to identify statistical anomalies that may represent a potential problem or to identify predictive behaviour patterns. In either case, data is modelled and analysed to provide some information, which is then interpreted through an evaluation procedure. This behaviour is described in the trading advisory system presented by Chu et al. [4], in which the system monitors and evaluates stock market data to identify specific movements in the market that may provide lucrative trading opportunities. The system uses various economic rules and principles as expert knowledge to assist traders in making decisions on ideal types of stocks to buy and sell.

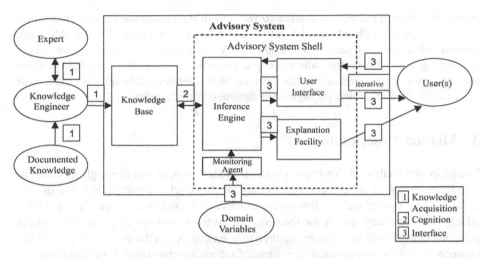

Fig. 1. Advisory System Architecture, presented in [1]

In the diagnosis and recovery style, parameters are manually input to the advisory system to frame a problem, where potential causes and/or solutions are automatically generated by the system from an analysis procedure. An example of advisory systems that adopt this style is described by Kassim and Abdullah [5]. Here, the advisory system is designed for use within agriculture is proposed for advising farmers on the most suitable rural areas and seasons in which to cultivate crops, as well as the types of crops that should be grown. Farmers provide the system with values for various input parameters to frame the problem, where expert knowledge is applied to infer possible solutions on which area a farmer is most likely to be successful and the types of crops that should be grown. In a final example, presented by Engrand and Mitchell [6], a set of advisory systems embedded in shuttle flight computer systems are described, where separate advisory systems are used for diagnosing malfunctions and handling faults. The user interacts with these systems to determine the cause of malfunctions and identify how these may be repaired. Data concerning the physical condition of the shuttle, is provided to these systems through the control system as a continuous stream, where there is an immediate need for the advisory systems to respond in real-time. Various other examples of applications are also described in [2, 3, 7–10].

As advisory systems continue to be applied to various industrial settings, where failures can potentially have serious effects, reliability and dependability become important factors. This is to ensure that the software is likely to continue its intended function, without errors, and under specific conditions over a period of time [17]. There are many examples of software reliability models in the literature that can be applied to predict or estimate reliability in the software applications, where these approaches can provide meaningful results [18]. However, ensuring reliability in software is difficult to achieve as a result of high complexity, where advisory systems are considered to be very complex systems. This is because, unlike conventional software, there is a knowledge base that is used to provide various parameters for deducing conclusions, where the margin for error is greater. This has been the main reason why considerable emphasis has been placed on ensuring correctness in the representation and application of knowledge through advanced V&V methods and techniques [13–16]. Although various advancements have been made, V&V in knowledge based systems is a developing area of research, where many approaches are still in their infancy. Consequently, the focus of reliability has received little attention, although, there is a clear need to ensure that advisory systems are designed for reliability.

3 Method Description

The proposed method in this paper aims to provide a simple and thorough approach in which the design of an advisory system may be effectively described, in terms of user requirements, operational (or functional) requirements and overall system structure – which is the primary reason for focusing on advisory systems from an architectural perspective as each of these can be captured to an extent. As for the design of each specific component, this is only considered in terms of the architectural style for that component and the types of mechanisms that are expected to be present in order for the functional requirements to be successfully addressed. In effect, this provides specific guidelines for the implementation of the system and can potentially be useful when developing a formal specification. The process model of the method is presented in Fig. 2.

As can be seen from the diagram, the first process is the documentation of the user, non-functional and functional requirements, which are encapsulated in the system requirements. It is also expected that the requirements specification would also consist of a high-level design concept in which to begin considering an appropriate software

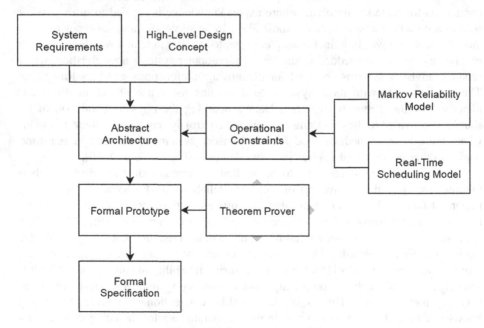

Fig. 2. Method process model

solution. The next phase is the development of an abstract architecture that lists each of the core components for the system, with suitable descriptions of the function of these – particularly in terms of input and generated output, dependencies and basic function. This allows the designer to consider the structure of each component in which such functions may be achieved, which can easily be represented through a state machine. These state machines begin to become connected as dependencies are introduced into the model, which establishes an architectural model. This can be extended by simply translating the architectural model into a Markov model, where probabilities of state transitions are defined. To ensure reliability, operational constraints are also used to extend the model which to define specific conditions that must be adhered to in order to ensure successful state transitions for the majority of cases. This can be in terms of ensuring the correct input format, defining conditions of failure and conditions for recovery.

It is appreciated that not every advisory system will be required to perform in real-time, therefore inclusion of a real-time scheduling model is optional. The purpose of this is to simply set deadlines for each component and conditions for execution time.

With a description of the architectural model, it is then translated into a formal simulation prototype in which each of the constraints may be proven in concept, ensuring that there are no deadlocks, the system performs in accordance to the original requirements that were documented and performs correctly. Essentially, the formal prototype is to ensure correctness of the constraints in terms of their ability to satisfy the reliability criteria, which to ensure proof of termination, proof of correctness (which respect to requirements) and proof of real-time – which, at the design phase, can only be achieved in theory.

4 System Requirements and Design Concept

Given the description of the method, as described in the previous section, the remainder of this paper considers the application to an active research project concerned with the design and development of next generation advisory systems. The requirements and design concept that is described in this section is for an advisory system that has been designed for use within the railway domain. The design and development of this system is the focus of an ongoing PhD project that is sponsored by Siemens Rail Automation and the Engineering and Physical Sciences Research Council (EPSRC). The purpose of this system is to identify ongoing or potential delays in an area of the railway network that is monitored by the traffic control system and to advise the traffic coordinator, as the decision-maker, on possible rescheduling strategies that may be applied to allow for (partial) recovery of a delay or to avoid potential future delays. The advisory system, in this context, is required to ensure that a reasonable degree of dependability in the railway network is maintained. This objective is motivated by active demands within the railway industry for systems that can provide automated support, particularly for dispatchers, who are mainly responsible for managing delays. Currently, dispatchers often rely on experience and intuition to make predictions of a train's arrival time to a station based on the last known delays that were recorded and the train's relative position. This method, as discussed in Martin [12], is considered imprecise since it does not account for partial recoveries or extended delays as it assumes that a train would maintain its current trajectory. A level of automation is therefore necessary to ensure improved accuracy in predictions of train arrival and departure times for each controllable point in its path. The potential of this proposed advisory system is the degree in which operational reliability may be improved by providing dispatchers with more accurate information, which can be incorporated in planning and re-planning processes.

The user requirements for this system are particularly extensive, especially in terms of human-computer interactions. However, the key requirements are that the advisory system must extend the functionality of current operational control systems, such as the European Traffic Control System (ETCS), by providing advice that ensures robustness of the original timetable when disruptions to services occur. This directly states that all advice should be produced for the purpose of recommending a rerouting strategy for any disrupted services to ensure that each train is capable of arriving as close to the original timetabled deadline as possible. A delay of up to a maximum of 10 min is generally acceptable. The advice is also expected to be produced in real-time, which has been specifically defined as a time period between 2–5 min. This is to allow time for decision to be made by the traffic coordinator, dispatcher or signal operator. Finally, the advice itself must be robust enough to ensure that any unintentional delays do not occur. This means that if a potential or ongoing delay has been recognized at a point in time in a specific section of the railway network, the advice should not list any suggestions that are likely to cause a delay later in the future. Other requirements also include enabling the user the easily understand and interpret the advice that is produced, where delays and problems can instantly be recognized and initiate the contingency planning process that takes place to accommodate for expected disruptions, as well provide some prompts on actions that may be taken to minimizes the effect of the disruption.

5   System Architecture

The abstract architecture, which implements the specification, for the rail advisory system, as illustrated in Fig. 3, is structured into four major components, which are the knowledge base, the inference engine, the data processing agent (or monitoring agent) and the interface. This architecture is based on the general advisory system architecture and the system concepts that were presented by Beemer and Gregg [1], where it has been modified specifically for addressing the key requirements outlined in the previous section.

As with general advisory systems, the role of the knowledge base is to simply store domain specific knowledge that is referenced by the inference engine, which frames the problem and identifies possible solutions that are both presented to the user via the interface. The inference engine is constructed from three main algorithmic subcomponents, which are the prediction, rescheduling and advice generation algorithms.

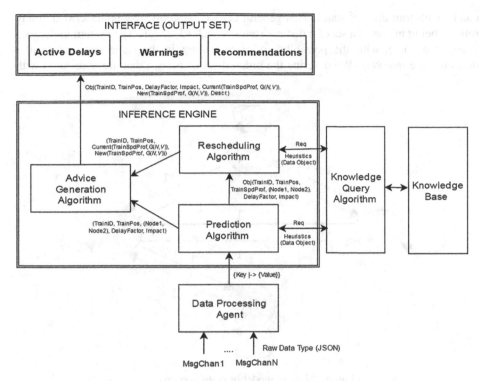

Fig. 3. Abstract architecture of the rail advisory system with data flow annotations

Respectively, these algorithms: receive information from the data processing agent to predict possible train delays that are likely to occur as well as to predict the potential impact of delays that are either ongoing or are likely; to use the predicted impact as a value for a cost metric to define cost of paths, where the cheapest and most feasible path is identified; and to use information of possible delays, the effects of these and the most suitable path(s) to generate understandable advice for the user. The advice generation algorithm is also expected to cross check the advice against previous advice to ensure that the results are consistent. To ensure speed in processing, there is separate driver algorithm that extracts specific information from the knowledge base to provide the necessary heuristics that are required by both the prediction and the rescheduling algorithms. Finally, the data processing agent is responsible for extracting raw data from the control system and to process it to identify key statistical and stochastic information that can be used for prediction.

5.1 Markov Reliability Model

The Markov model consists of a list of the possible states of the advisory system, the possible transition paths between those states and the rate parameters of those transitions [16]. Figure 4 presents a Markov state machine (sometimes called a Markov chain) with four distinct states. This general class of systems may be described at any time as being in one of a set of n distinct states, s1, s2, s3, ..., sn. The system undergoes changes of state, with the possibility of it remaining in the same state, at regular discrete time intervals. We describe the ordered set of times t that are associated with

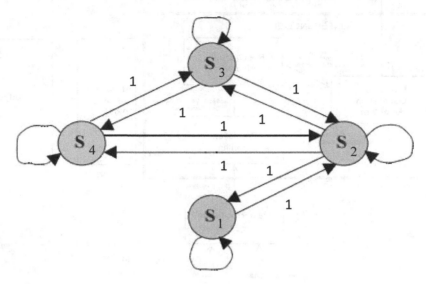

Fig. 4. Markov model of cognition process

the discrete intervals as t1, t2, t3, ..., tn. The system changes state according to the distribution of probabilities associated with each state. We denote the actual state of the machine at time t as st. The states represent the following: S1 is data processing; s2 is prediction; s3 is knowledge query and s4 is rescheduling.

A full probabilistic description of this system requires, in the general case, the specification of the present state *st*, in terms of all its predecessor states. Thus, the probability of the system being in any particular state *st* is: $p(st) = p(st \mid st - 1, st - 2, st - 3, ...)$ where the *st − 1* are the predecessor states of *st*. In a first-order Markov chain, the probability of the present state is a function only of its direct predecessor state: $p(st) = p(st \mid st - 1)$ where *st − 1* is the predecessor of *st*. We next assume that the right side of this equation is time invariant, that is, we hypothesise that across all time periods of the system, the transitions between specific states retain the same probabilistic relationships. Based on these assumptions, we now can create a set of state transition probabilities aij between any two states si and sj as follows: $aij = p(st = si \mid st - 1 = sj)$, $1 \geq i, j \geq N$ Note that i can equal j, in which case the system remains in the same state. The traditional constraints remain on these probability distributions; for each state si: N aij ≥ 0, and for all j, Σ aij = 1 i = 1. The system we have just described is called a first-order observable Markov model since the output of the system is the set of states at each discrete time interval. The transition probabilities are observed from the operational profile and are independent of component reliabilities. If component ci connects to n subsequent components { i k c | 1≤ k ≤ n }, the transition probability Pij between components ci and i j c is equal to $\sum = n\, k\, t\, i\, j\, t\, i\, k\, 1$ (,) (,). Here, t(i,j) is the total number of invocations or control transfers from component ci to i j c. In this section, we describe reliability modeling of software with single architectural style. For simplicity, the connector reliabilities will not be considered until the modeling of heterogeneous architecture in the next section. Four architectural styles are used to demonstrate how to model reliability of software with single architectural style. These styles include batch-sequential, parallel/pipe-filter, call-and-return, and fault tolerance styles.

5.2 Real-Time Scheduling Model

The performance criteria of the advisory system is classified as firm, where each component must perform according to a firm deadline. The term *firm* is used as the system must produce an output that is important for ensuring the dependability of the railway, however, complete failure to produce on time is expected to result in inconvenience and loss of productivity, rather a failure in the railway. There are many mathematical models available to represent scheduling that are used to implement scheduling algorithms. For the purpose of this paper, we refer to a simple static scheduling model, where each component in the advisory system, except for the knowledge base, performs a process that is described as being a sequence of tasks. The schedule is an assignment of the tasks to be processed so that each task is able to execute until completion. In the case study, it has been explicitly stated from potential end-users that a best execution time is any time that less than, or equal to 2 min. The worst case execution time was stated as being at most 5 min. Any advice that was produced after 5 min would not be considered useful as it would require the dispatcher at least 10 min to make a decision, where 15 min would have elapsed before any decision was made and implemented, by which time the situation may be different given the constantly changing state of the railway network. In particular, time periods of up to 20 min in European national railway lines is considered significant as this the minimum time required to observe any real change in state [11]. The average execution time, therefore, would be any time between 2 and 5 min. The schedule for each component. Development of the scheduling model is described in detail in [19], where we simply use the preemptive fixed priority scheduling model to assess the feasibility of developing a fixed priority schedule. Here, each component is to execute according to a priority, where the data processing has the highest priority until execution, where prediction has the next highest priority. Each component must perform according to a deadline, where we evenly distribute the time for each component, where the best case for each is 30 s and the worst is 1 min. The performance time of the system is the sum of execution of each component, where if it is proven that each component can perform to the deadline, then the system can also perform against the deadline as well.

Whist the work described in [19] is very important, it is not complete in the sense that it ignores the impact of the time required to perform system tasks. And there are reasons to believe that such overhead in not negligible, since interrupt handling, task switching and preemption are vital to fixed priority scheduling and may occur frequently. Two implementations are possible for a fixed priority scheduler [19]: event-driven and time-driven. In event-driven scheduling, all tasks are initiated by internal or external events.

6 SPARK Prototype

This section presents the final phase of the formal design method, in which the abstract architecture and operational constraints are implemented for the purpose of defining a formal prototype. The aim of the prototype is to conduct various simulations to ensure correct operational behaviour, mainly in terms of real-time execution and data flow control. As the operational constraints are captured to describe correct operational behaviour, it is important that these are proven for correctness using V&V and are formally expressed, which is achieved using SPARK.

SPARK is based on the principle of Correctness by Construction, an efficient and mathematically rigorous approach to software development that avoids defects, or detects and removes them quickly. Correctness by Construction involves strong static verification as the system is being implemented and allows the cumulative develop ment of certification-oriented evidence.

SPARK is an Ada subset augmented with a notation for specifying contracts (annotations in the form of Ada comments) that are analysed statically. The current version of SPARK is based on Ada 2005 and includes a large portion of Ada's static semantic facilities such as packages/encapsulation, subprograms, most types, and some Object-Oriented Programming features, as well as the Ravenscar tasking profile. Features such as exceptions, goto statements, and dynamic binding are excluded because they would complicate formal verification; other features such as access types (*pointers*), dynamically sized arrays, and recursion are excluded because they would interfere with time or space predictability.

Below is a brief example of the coded implementation used in building the prototype, which focuses specifically in controlling the execution of tasks by stopping and starting them in response to events that occur. Each event is scheduled according to a specified deadline, where a simple scheduling algorithm is implemented. For simplicity, the tasks

```
package Task_Control
is
   type Suspension_Object is limited private;

   procedure Set_True(S
: in out Suspension_Object);
   --# derives S from ;
   -- Note the apparent mismatch between the parameter mode and
the derives annotation^R4.
   -- This arises because the Ada run-time system needs to
read SO in order to determine
   -- whether any tasks should now be started whereas, for flow
analysis purposes, we only
   -- need to record the fact that SO is given a new value that does
not depend on any import.

   procedure Set_False(S
: in out Suspension_Object);
   --# derives S from ;

   procedure Suspend_Until_True(S
: in out Suspension_Object);
   --# derives S from ;

private
   --# hide Task_Control;
  end Task_Control;

....

sub-
type Any_Priority        is Integer        range
0 .. 31;
sub-
type Priority            is Any_Priority range
0 .. 30;
sub-
type Interrupt_Priority is Any_Priority range 3
1 .. 31;
```

Program 1: Program extract for task control and priority scheduling

This code extract is applied to the scheduling algorithm to specify tasks, and the order of tasks, that are to be scheduled. The result of the code is that very abstract definitions of tasks, which simply represent data processing, knowledge query, prediction and rescheduling, are scheduled, where the task control extract ensures that the next task proceeds when the previous task has completely executed. The priority of scheduling changes after the completion of each task, where initially data processing has the highest priority and after its completion, the prediction and knowledge query are then given priority. The algorithm iterates in a cycle to represent a continuous stream of data that is provided to the advisory system and performs over 100000 iterations before terminating.

The final coded solution also includes various procedures that regulate data flow control, particularly in terms of ensuring that each component, as a defined process, sends and receives data in the correct format, which is defined as an object for simplicity, and that the data object is initialised with some value. If the value is null an exception is thrown and the process is unable to complete, however, to ensure that the system doesn't crash, the final output is simply an exception message.

7 Conclusions

This paper proposed a formal design method for designing reliable advisory systems, where the basic concepts of this were presented. The results that were accumulated demonstrated some potential in applying this approach to the development of a formal specification of industrial advisory systems in settings where reliability and dependability are important requirements. The development of this method, and improvement thereof, is an ongoing work, where there are many avenues in which to improve that will be explored in the future. A key concern in this approach, which is to be addressed in subsequent work, is that while the method aims to provide a thorough design for reliability and evaluation of the design, there is a risk that too much time can be spent in developing expressive models. It is important that the reliability models capture as much detail as possible, in terms of component dependencies and execution deadlines. However, significant levels of abstraction are required to develop these models and capture the operational constraints. It is felt that the description is an oversimplified view of the system and, therefore, may be limited in its practical use. This is especially true when developing the formal prototype. Although, it is useful in demonstrating the relationship between each component, the order of execution, expected time period of execution and data control procedures.

In terms of real-time performance, it is not possible to identify if a component will be able to perform in real-time solely by its abstract specification. This is because concrete specifications and algorithm designs are typically analysed to estimate realtime capability, which are not available from an architectural perspective. A difficulty is that the architectural style of many components, defined by the specification, are fault-tolerant – which impacts on real-time performance as recovery processes can be costly in execution time. However, some processes are also concurrent and a predictable finite process model is defined, which provides some confidence of real-time execution at an architectural level. At this stage, it is believed to be possible to extend the constraints of the process model by defining a scheduling model. A more accurate estimate, however, and indeed a proof, can be derived from the analysis of the algorithms that are used and empirical evidence can be gathered post-implementation. Nevertheless, time constraints are defined and incorporated into the model, where a predictable and deterministic performance is required to ensure that these constraints are met.

References

1. Beemer, B.A., Gregg, D.G.: Advisory systems to support decision making. In: Handbook on Decision Support Systems 1: Basic Themes, 2007, chapt. 24, pp. 361–377. Springer (2007)
2. Fensel, D., Groenboom, R.: A software architecture for knowledge-based systems. Knowl. Eng. Rev. **14**(2), 153–173 (1999)
3. Dunkel, J., Bruns, R.: Software architecture of advisory systems using agent and semantic web technologies. In: Proceedings of the 2005 IEEE/WIC/ACM International Conference on Web Intelligence (WI 2005), pp. 418–421 (2005)
4. ElAlfi, A.E.E., ElAlami, M.E.: Intelligent advisory system for supporting university managers in law. Int. J. Comput. Sci. Inf. Secur. (IJCSIS) **3**(1), 123–128 (2009)
5. Chu, S.C.W., Ng, H.S., Lam, K.P.: Intelligent trading advisor. In: Proceedings of the 2000 IEEE International Conference on Management of Innovation Technology, pp. 53–58 (2000)
6. Kassim, J.M., Abdullah, R.: Advisory system architecture in agricultural environment to support decision making process. In: 2nd International Conference on Digital Information and Communication Technology and its Applications, pp. 453–456 (2012)
7. Mburu, C., Lee, H., Mbogho, A.: E-Health advisory system for HIV/AIDS patients in South Africa. In: 7th International Conference on Appropriate Healthcare Technologies for Developing Countries, IET, pp. 1–4 (2012)
8. Engrand, P., Mitchell, T., Fowler, T., Melichar, T.: The development of a dvisory systems for shuttle slight computer systems at the kennedy space center. In: IEEE International Conference on Systems, Man and Cybernetics Conference Proceedings 1991, vol. 3, pp. 1685–1690 (1991)
9. Sadek, A.W.: Artificial Intelligence Applications in Trans portation. Artificial Intelligence in Transportation: Information for Application, Transportation Research Circular, No. E -C113, Transportation Research Board of the National Academies, pp. 1–6 (2007)
10. Spring, G.: Knowledge-based systems in transportation. Artificial Intelligence in Transportation: Information for Application, Transportation Research Circular, No. E-C113, Transportation Research Board of the National Academies, 2007, pp. 7–16 (2007)
11. Martin, L.J.: Predictive reasoning and machine learning for the enhancement of reliability in railway systems. In: Lecomte, T., Pinger, R., Romanovsky, A. (eds.) RSSRail 2016. LNCS, vol. 9707, pp. 178–188. Springer, Heidelberg (2016). doi:10.1007/978-3-319-33951-1_13
12. Ayel, M., Laurent, J.P.: Validation, verification and test of knowledge-based systems. IEEE Trans. Knowl. Data Eng. **11**(1), 292–312 (1999)
13. Serrano, J.A.: Formal specifications of software design methods. In: IW-FM 1999 Proceedings of the 3rd Irish Conference on Formal Methods, British Computer Society, Swindon, UK, pp. 208–224 (1999)
14. Meseguer, P., Preece, A.D.: Verification and validation of knowledge-based systems with formal specifications. Knowl. Eng. Rev. **4**(1) (1995)
15. Antoniou, G., van Harmelen, F., Plant, R., Vanthienen, J.: Verification and validation of knowledge-based systems. AI Mag. **19**(3), 123–126 (1998)
16. Tsai, W.T., Vishnuvajjala, R., Zhang, D.: Verification and validation of knowledge-based systems. IEEE Trans. Knowl. Data Eng. **11**(1), 202–212 (1999)
17. Kitchin, J.F.: Practical markov modelling for reliability analysis. In: Proceedings of the Annual Reliability and Maintainability Symposium, pp. 290–296 (1988)

18. Wang, W.L., Pan, D., Chen, M.H.: Architecture-based software reliability modeling. J. Syst. Softw. **79**(1), 132–146 (2006)
19. de Magalhães, A.J.P., Costa, C.J.A.: Real-Time Scheduling Models. Technical report, Controlo 2000, 4th Portuguese Conference on Automatic Control (2000)
20. Dross, C., Efstathopoulos, P., Lesens, D., Mentré, D., Moy, Y.: Rail, space, security: three case studies for SPARK 2014. In: Proceedings of the ERTS (2014)

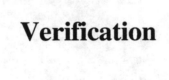

Verification

Verifying Multi-core Schedulability
with Data Decision Diagrams

Dimitri Racordon[✉] and Didier Buchs

Centre Universitaire d'Informatique, University of Geneva, Geneva, Switzerland
{dimitri.racordon,didier.buchs}@unige.ch

Abstract. Over the past few years, numerous real-time and embedded systems have been adopting multi-core architectures for either better performances, or energy efficiency. For the case of real-time applications, where tasks can have critical deadlines, it is desirable to ensure the schedulability of the application statically, taking into account the possible software and hardware failures. While a lot of effort have been made to handle software misbehaviours, resilience to hardware failures has often been overlooked.

In this paper, we propose to study the schedulability of multi-core applications. Specifically, we want to check statically whether or not a real-time system will be able to meet the deadlines of its most critical tasks, even when one or more of its cores are offline. In order to achieve this goal, we translate the schedulability problem into a state space exploration, using Data Decision Diagrams to support the computation and analysis of such state space.

1 Introduction

Multi-core architectures appear to have been the ultimate answer to the constant increase of computational power required by modern applications. Over the past few years, numerous real-time and embedded systems have been adopting those architectures for either better performances, or energy efficiency. This shift introduced new challenges to be met, as to provide efficient and reliable scheduling methods. In particular for the case of real-time applications, it is desirable to ensure the schedulability of the application statically, taking into account timing and energy constraints, as well as possible software and hardware failures. While a lot of effort have been made to handle software misbehaviours [3], resilience to hardware failures has often been overlooked.

In this paper, we propose to address this issue by verifying the schedulability of multi-core systems, with respect to core failures. Specifically, we want to check statically whether or not a real-time system will be able to meet the deadlines of its most critical tasks, even when one or more of its cores are offline. In order to achieve this goal, our approach consists of translating the schedulability problem into a state space exploration, thus enabling us to use well-proven model checking techniques to compute and examine very large state spaces. Namely, we build the set of all possible schedulings so we can check if at least one of them satisfies

© Springer International Publishing Switzerland 2016
I. Crnkovic and E. Troubitsyna (Eds.): SERENE 2016, LNCS 9823, pp. 45–61, 2016.
DOI: 10.1007/978-3-319-45892-2_4

a set of properties, despite one or more core failures. We represent this *scheduling space* in a Data Decision Diagram (DDD), a very compact structure that have been successfully used to tackle large software verification problems [12].

The remaining of this paper is organized as follows. Section 2 gives an overview of related literature. Section 3 defines the schedulability problem. Section 4 introduces DDDs and the operations we will use to manipulate them. Sections 5 and 6 respectively describe our translation of the schedulability problem into a state space exploration, and the schedulability properties of such state space. Section 7 presents our experimental results. Finally, concluding remarks and future works are given in Sect. 8.

2   Related Literature

One angle of schedulability analysis is the study of *mode changes*. A system is either in its *normal mode* in the absence of failure, and switches to a *degraded mode* when a failure occurs. Our work fits very well into this category, as we seek to statically verify the schedulability of the tasks of a system (or its most critical ones) in *degraded mode*, after a core failure. A similar approach was studied by Baruah and Guo, who proposed a formal framework to model degradation in processor speed [1]. However, they focused on single-core architectures, while we support multi-core architectures as well.

A more prominent approach to schedulability analysis is the use of time and/or space redundancy [15]. In the former, a task is executed multiple times on the same core while in the latter, it is executed on different cores. In both cases, the results produced by the multiple copies are then compared to spot and hopefully correct potential errors. In [5], Cirinei et al. proposed a technique to allow the software designer to tune the trade-off between parallelism and fault-tolerance, so as to guarantee the schedulability of a subset of critical tasks in the event of a transient error. In the same area, Pathan proposed an algorithm to compute the minimum number of cores required by a system to be schedulable, with respect to a maximum number of transient errors [17]. More recently, Nikolic et al. improved on the aforementioned works to study permanent core failures as well [16]. However, these approaches focus solely on the timing constraints, whereas our method can also consider other constraints, such as the energy consumption.

With respect to the representation of the scheduling problem with decision diagrams, Jensen et al. proposed to compute the state space of schedulings with Binary Decision Diagrams (BDDs) [11]. However, their model only supports homogeneous architectures, whereas ours can also support heterogeneous architectures. More recently, Cire and Hoeve proposed to use Multi-Valued Decision Diagrams (MDDs) to optimise the decision of a scheduler [4], but their method focuses on finding an optimal scheduling, rather than determining the schedulability.

3   The Schedulability Problem

In this section, we define the schedulability problem for multi-core architectures. We first define our task model. Then we formulate the schedulability problem as to determine whether or not there exists at least one scheduling respecting the task model constraints.

3.1   The Task Model

Let $T = \{t_1, \ldots, t_n\}$ be a finite set of tasks. A function μ associates a quadruple $\langle r, c, d, k \rangle$ to each task $t \in T$, where $r \in \mathbb{N}$ denotes its release time (i.e. the earliest time it is available to be processed), $c \in \mathbb{N}$ denotes its worst case execution time, $d \in \mathbb{N}$ denotes its deadline (i.e. the latest time it should finish), and $k \in \mathbb{N}$ denotes its criticality level. If $\mu(t) = \langle r, c, d, k \rangle$, we write $\mu_r(t) = r$, $\mu_c(t) = c$, $\mu_d(t) = d$ and $\mu_k(t) = k$. Let $\prec \subseteq T \times T$ denote the dependency relationship between the tasks, such that $t \prec u$ means that u can only start after t was executed. This relation is transitive, i.e. $\forall t, u, v \in T, t \prec u \wedge u \prec v \implies t \prec v$. Given a dependency relationship $\prec$, we write $\mathcal{D}(t) = \{u \in T \mid u \prec t\}$ the set of tasks t depends on. We do not allow dependency cycles, i.e. $\forall t \in T, t \notin \mathcal{D}(t)$. Finally, we define our task model:

Definition 1. *A task model is triple* $\mathcal{M} = \langle T, \mu, \prec \rangle$ *where T is a finite set of tasks, μ is a function that gives the task constraints and $\prec$ is the dependency relationship between the tasks.*

Remark 1. A task model $\mathcal{M} = \langle T, \mu, \prec \rangle$ can be seen as a directed acyclic graph $G = \langle T, E \rangle$ where $E \subseteq \{(t, u) \in T \times T \mid t \prec u\}$ denote the direct dependencies, and where each node $t \in T$ is annotated with $\mu(t)$.

Figure 1 gives an example of a task model consisting of five tasks, represented as a graph. Tasks t_0, t_2 and t_4 do not have any dependencies, while t_1 depends on t_0 and t_2, and t_3 depends on t_1, in addition to t_0 and t_2 by transitivity. The constraints of the tasks μ are given as node annotations. For instance, $\mu(t_1) = \langle 4, 2, 10, 0 \rangle$, meaning that it will be released at time 4, takes at most 2 units of time to be executed, must be completed before time 10 and has criticality level 0.

Note that our model is very similar to the one described in [3]. The main difference lies in the fact that their model handles what they call *sporadic tasks*, which must be executed periodically. This can give rise to unbounded sequences of tasks and cannot be handled by our state space exploration. However, if we restrict ourselves to a time window, we can explicitly enumerate all occurrences of sporadic tasks. For instance, the tasks t_0, t_2 and t_4 of Fig. 1 could be seen as a single sporadic task released every 4 units of time.

3.2   The Schedulability Problem

Let $\mathcal{C} = \{c_1, \ldots, c_n\}$ be a finite set of cores. We can define a scheduling as follows:

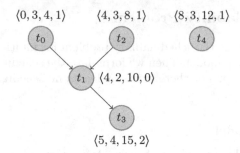

$\langle 0, 3, 4, 1 \rangle$ $\langle 4, 3, 8, 1 \rangle$ $\langle 8, 3, 12, 1 \rangle$

t_0 t_2 t_4

t_1 $\langle 4, 2, 10, 0 \rangle$

t_3

$\langle 5, 4, 15, 2 \rangle$

Fig. 1. Example of a task model consisting of 5 tasks.

Definition 2. *Given a task model* $\mathcal{M} = \langle T, \mu, \prec \rangle$ *and a set of cores* $\mathcal{C}$, *a scheduling is a partial function* $S : T \rightarrow \mathcal{C} \times \mathbb{N}$ *that assigns a task to a core at a specific starting time.*

If $S(t) = \langle c, \tau \rangle$, we write $S_c(t) = c$ and $S_\tau(t) = \tau$. Note that the above definition does not require a scheduling to assign all task, nor to respect all task constraints. We say that a scheduling is *feasible* if it does, and we define it as follows:

Definition 3. *A scheduling* S *is feasible for* $\mathcal{M}$ *and* $\mathcal{C}$ *if and only if:*

- *all tasks are scheduled after their dependencies finished their execution,*
  i.e. $\forall t \in T, \forall u \in \mathcal{D}(t), S_\tau(u) + \mu_c(u) \leq S_\tau(t)$
- *all tasks are scheduled after their release time,*
  i.e. $\forall t \in T, S_\tau(t) \geq \mu_r(t)$
- *all deadlines are met,*
  i.e. $\forall t \in T, S_\tau(t) + \mu_c(t) \leq \mu_d(t)$

Definition 4. *A scheduling* S *is consistent if and only if there are no tasks scheduled on the same core at the same time, i.e.*
$\forall t, u \in T, t \neq u \wedge S_c(t) = S_c(u) \wedge S_\tau(t) \leq S_\tau(u) \implies S_\tau(t) + \mu_c(t) \leq S_\tau(u)$

The schedulability problem consists in determining whether or not there exists at least one feasible and consistent scheduling, given a task model $\mathcal{M}$ and a set of cores $\mathcal{C}$.

Figure 2 shows two examples of scheduling for the task model of Fig. 1. The scheduling on the left considers a two-core architecture. It is feasible, since it

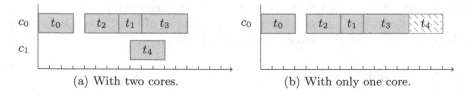

| c_0 | t_0 | t_2 | t_1 | t_3 |

| c_1 | t_4 |

(a) With two cores.

| c_0 | t_0 | t_2 | t_1 | t_3 | t_4 |

(b) With only one core.

Fig. 2. Two examples of schedulings.

respects all tasks constraints and dependencies, and consistent since it does not schedule more than one task on a given core, at a given time. The scheduling on the right considers a one-core architecture. It is also consistent but is not feasible, since it does not respect the deadline of t_4 (hatched in the figure). Note that the gap between t_0 and t_2 is introduced by the release time of t_2.

There exist two kinds of schedulers, namely *preemptive* ones which can pause a running task to execute another one instead, and *cooperative* ones which cannot. For the sake of simplicity, we will focus on the latter in this paper

3.3 k-relaxed Schedulability

It is not hard to see that the task model of Fig. 1 is actually not schedulable on a one-core architecture. The reason is that it is not possible to schedule t_3 on time without making t_4 late, and vice versa. One way to tackle this problem is to relax our definition of feasibility to consider only the most critical tasks. In our model, t_3 is more critical than t_4. Hence, it could be reasonable to give priority to t_3, and forget about t_4. This could be seen as a kind of *degraded mode*, in which we only care about the most critical tasks until the system can be restored.

Given a task model $\mathcal{M} = \langle T, \mu, \prec \rangle$, we say that a task t is k-critical if either its criticality level $\mu_k(t)$ is greater or equal to k, or if one its dependencies is k-critical. We define $T_{\geq k} = \{t \in T \mid \exists u \in \{t\} \cup \mathcal{D}(t), \mu_k(u) \geq k\}$ as the set of k-critical tasks, and we say that a scheduling $S_{\geq k}$ is k-feasible if and only if it is feasible for all tasks in $T_{\geq k}$. Finally, we can define the k-relaxed schedulability problem as determining whether or not there exists at least one k-feasible and consistent scheduling, given a task model $\mathcal{M}$ and a set of cores $\mathcal{C}$.

Back to our task model example, we can now see that Fig. 2b depicts a 2-feasible and consistent scheduling.

4   Data Decision Diagrams

Data Decision Diagrams were introduced by Couvreur et al. in [7] as a data structure capable of representing large sets of sequences of assignments of discrete values (as opposed to BDDs that represents sequences of binary assignments [2]). They take advantage of the similarities between those sequences to compact their representation in a graph-like structure, and are also equipped with a class of operators called homomorphisms that can manipulate them.

4.1   Definition of Data Decision Diagrams

A DDD is a directed acyclic graph where non-terminal nodes correspond to a variable in a given set E, terminal nodes denote the existence or absence of a sequence in the represented set, and edges correspond to the value $x \in dom(e)$ a variable $e \in E$ can take. Hence, a path from the root to a terminal indicates whether a particular sequence of assignments $\langle e_1 = x_1, \ldots, e_n = x_n \rangle$ where

$e_1, \ldots, e_n \in E$ and $x_1 \in dom(e_1), \ldots, x_n \in dom(e_n)$ exists in the represented set. Namely, if the path ends on the terminal 0, then the sequence does not exist; if it ends on the terminal 1, then sequence does exist. For the purpose of this paper, we assume that E is a finite set equipped with a total ordering $< \subseteq E \times E$. We assume that $\forall e \in E, dom(e)$ is discrete, but not necessarily finite. We write $E_< = [e_1, \ldots, e_n]$ the ordered sequence such that $n = |E|$ and $\forall e_i, e_j \in E_<, i < j \implies e_i < e_j$. Then we define the set of DDDs inductively as follows:

Definition 5. *Let E be a finite set of variables and $n = |E|$. The set of DDDs $\mathbb{D}$ is the union of all $\mathbb{D}_i$ for $0 \le i \le n$ where:*

- *$\mathbb{D}_0 = \{0, 1\}$*
- *$\forall e_i \in E_<, \mathbb{D}_i = \{(e_i, \alpha) \mid \alpha : dom(e_i) \to \mathbb{D}_{i-1}$ and $\text{supp}(\alpha)$ is finite$\}$*

with $\text{supp}(\alpha) = \{x \in dom(e) \mid \alpha(x) \neq 0\}$ for some $e \in E$.

Note that this definition implies that for any node in a DDD, all successor nodes represent either the assignments of smaller variables, or a terminal symbol. We write $e \xrightarrow{x} d$ the DDD $(e, \alpha) \in \mathbb{D}$ where $\alpha(x) = d$ and for all $y \neq x, \alpha(y) = 0$.

Because all paths ending on the terminal 0 represent the empty set of sequences of assignment, there is an infinite number of representations for it if $\exists e \in E, dom(e)$ is infinite. Therefore, we introduce the notion of *vanishing terminal*, as proposed in [13].

Definition 6. *Let $0 \in \mathbb{D}$ be vanishing. $\alpha \in \mathbb{D}_i$ is vanishing if and only if $\forall x \in dom(e_i), \alpha(x)$ is vanishing.*

As a result, we can reduce any DDD to its most compact representation by removing all vanishing nodes and edges leading to them.

Figure 3 presents three examples of DDDs. The total ordering on E is given by $c < b < a$. All three DDDs are canonical. The left DDD (Fig. 3a) encodes the following four sequences of assignments, namely $\langle a = 0, b = 2, c = 2 \rangle$, $\langle a = 0, b = 2, c = 6 \rangle$, $\langle a = 3, b = 4, c = 2 \rangle$ and $\langle a = 3, b = 4, c = 6 \rangle$.

4.2   Operations on Data Decision Diagrams

DDDs support all usual set-theoretic operations, i.e. the union, the product and the difference. For the purpose of this paper, we will only describe the union. Please refer to [7] for the two others.

Definition 7. *The union $\cup$ of two DDDs is defined inductively as follows:*

- *$1 \cup 1 = 1$*
- *$\forall d \in \mathbb{D}_i, 0 \cup d = d \cup 0 = d$*
- *$\forall (e_1, \alpha_1), (e_2, \alpha_2) \in \mathbb{D}_i, (e_1, \alpha_1) \cup (e_2, \alpha_2) = (e_1, \alpha_1 \cup \alpha_2,$ where $\forall x \in dom(e_i), (\alpha_1 \cup \alpha_2)(x) = \alpha_1(x) \cup \alpha_2(x)$*

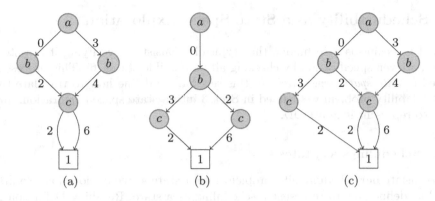

Fig. 3. Three examples of a DDDs.

Note that we do not define the union for DDDs of different lengths (except for empty set 0), so as to avoid incompatibilities between variable orderings.

The DDD of Fig. 3c is equivalent to the union of those of Fig. 3a and b. In other words, it represents all their sequences of assignments.

In addition to the union operation, we introduce the notion of homomorphism, so as to allow the definition of specific operations on the DDDs:

Definition 8. *A homomorphism is a mapping* $\Phi : \mathbb{D} \to \mathbb{D}$ *such that* $\Phi(0) \equiv 0$ *and* $\forall d_1, d_2 \in \mathbb{D}, \Phi(d_1 \cup d_2) = \Phi(d_1) \cup \Phi(d_2)$.

We define two homomorphisms, namely the identity id, as $\forall d \in \mathbb{D}, id(d) = d$, and the fixed point $\star$, as $\Phi^\star(d) = \Phi^n(d)$ where Φ is any homomorphism and n is the smallest integer such that $\Phi^n = \Phi^{n-1}$. Other specific operations can be defined as *inductive homomorphisms*. For those, it is sufficient to define $\Phi(1) \in \mathbb{D}$ and $\Phi(e, x)$ as a homomorphism (possibly inductive as well), for any $(e, x) \in E \times dom(e)$. Then, the application of an inductive homomorphism on (e, α) is given by:

$$\Phi((e, \alpha)) = \bigcup_{x \in dom(e)} \Phi'(e, x)(\alpha(x))$$

Example 1. Consider the following inductive homomorphisms that increments the value assigned to the variable $e_1 \in E$:

$$inc(e_1)(e, x) = \begin{cases} e \xrightarrow{x+1} id & \text{if } e = e_1 \\ e \xrightarrow{x} inc(e_1) & \text{otherwise} \end{cases}$$

$$inc(e_1)(1) = 1$$

Let us detail its application over a simple DDD:

$$inc(b)(a \xrightarrow{0} b \xrightarrow{3} c \xrightarrow{2} 1) = a \xrightarrow{0} inc(b)(b \xrightarrow{3} c \xrightarrow{2} 1)$$

$$= a \xrightarrow{0} b \xrightarrow{4} id(c \xrightarrow{2} 1)$$

$$= a \xrightarrow{0} b \xrightarrow{4} c \xrightarrow{2} 1$$

5   Schedulability as a State Space Exploration

Model Checking is a technique that typically consists of verifying if a system meets a given specification by checking all its possible states [6]. This process is called a *state space exploration*. In this section, we define how to translate the schedulability problem we defined in Sect. 3 into a state space exploration, and how to represent it in a DDD.

5.1   Schedulings as States

To translate our schedulability problem into a state space exploration, we first need to define how to represent a scheduling as a state. Recalling Definition 2, given a task model $\mathcal{M} = \langle T, \mu, \prec \rangle$ and a set of cores $\mathcal{C}$ a scheduling is a function $S : T \rightarrow \mathcal{C} \times \mathbb{N}$. If we write a scheduling as the cartesian product $T \times \mathcal{C} \times \mathbb{N}$, then the state space of schedulings is given by $A = \mathcal{P}(T \times \mathcal{C} \times \mathbb{N})$. As a result, given a set of tasks T and state space of schedulings A, the schedulability problem boils down to the existential quantification $\exists S \in A$ such that S is feasible and consistent for all tasks in T. Note that A is infinite, as long as neither T nor $\mathcal{C}$ is an empty set. However, as our schedulability problem states that we are interested in *feasible* schedulings only, we can bound the starting time of a task by the earliest release and latest possible starting time.

Lemma 1. *If we write a scheduling as the cartesian product $T \times \mathcal{C} \times \mathbb{N}$, then all feasible schedulings are members of the finite state space $A = \mathcal{P}(T \times \mathcal{C} \times \{\tau \mid \min_{t \in T}(\mu_{\mathrm{r}}(t)) \leq \tau \leq \max_{t \in T}(\mu_{\mathrm{d}}(t) - \mu_{\mathrm{c}}(t))\})$.*

Proof. A scheduling is feasible only if all tasks are scheduled after their release time. Hence, the earliest time any task can be scheduled cannot be smaller than the smallest release time amongst all tasks. Similarly, a scheduling is feasible only if all deadlines are met. Hence, the latest time any task can be scheduled cannot be greater than the greatest time a task can start and still meet its deadline, amongst all tasks.   ☐

5.2   Representing Schedulings in a DDD

Let $\mathcal{M} = \langle T, \mu, \prec \rangle$ be a task model and $\mathcal{C}$ a set of cores. For each core $c \in \mathcal{C}$, we associate a value $\tau \in \mathbb{N}$ that represents the next time the core is available. For each task $t \in T$ we associate either a tuple $\langle c, \tau \rangle \in \mathcal{C} \times \mathbb{N}$ or the value ϵ. The former indicates that the task t is scheduled on core c and will start at time τ. The latter simply means that the task is not scheduled yet. We use this value so that tasks can still be assigned to a value in the k-relaxed schedulings represented in a DDD.

Remark 2. Given a task model $\mathcal{M} = \langle T, \mu, \prec \rangle$ and a set of cores $\mathcal{C}$, we can represent a set of schedulings in a DDD where the set of variables E is given by $T \cup \mathcal{C}$, and the domains of variables are given by $\forall c \in \mathcal{C}, dom(c) = \mathbb{N}$ and $\forall t \in T, dom(t) = (\mathcal{C} \times \mathbb{N}) \cup \{\epsilon\}$.

The variable order can have a huge impact on the amount of shared nodes the DDD will have. Finding the order with the best sharing factor has been shown to be an NP-complete problem, and the motivation for numerous heuristics [8,18]. Defining a good heuristic for our schedulability problem is out of the scope of this paper, but a good rule of thumb is to place the core variables at the top, followed by the tasks ordered by how tight their constraints are (the tasks with the tightest constraints last). The rationale is that the fewer options there are to schedule a task, the more likely it is for it to be scheduled on the same core and at the same time on many schedulings. Similarly, the value assigned to the cores is likely to differ from one scheduling to another.

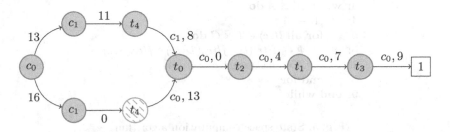

Fig. 4. Two schedulings represented as a DDD.

Figure 4 depicts a DDD that encodes the two schedulings we presented in Fig. 2. The path on the top encodes the scheduling on a two-core architecture, while that of the bottom is equivalent to a one-core architecture, where the second core is never used. The variable order is given by $t_3 < t_1 < t_2 < t_0 < t_4 < c_1 < c_0$ and is optimal for this problem. This order perfectly shares the identical part of both schedulings, which would not have been possible if we had swapped t_4 and t_3, for instance.

5.3   Computing the State Space

Roughly speaking, our state space computing method consists of iteratively refining the set of schedulings we have computed so far by trying to schedule more and more tasks, on every possible core. At each step, for each combination of task and core $\langle t, c \rangle$, we first filter out the schedulings, where t has already been scheduled, where the dependencies of t have not been executed yet and where it is not possible to satisfy the deadline of t. Then, we schedule t on c in all remaining schedulings at once, before we move on to the next pair. Let $A_0 = c_1 \xrightarrow{0} c_2 \xrightarrow{0} \ldots t_1 \xrightarrow{\epsilon} t_2 \xrightarrow{\epsilon} \ldots 1$ be the DDD representing the singleton composed of a scheduling where no task is scheduled. Then, our state space computation can be summarized as the algorithm presented in Fig. 5. As we can see, this algorithm corresponds to a fixed point computation on the set of schedulings A. Line 6 generates all the aforementioned filters and line 7 refines the remaining schedulings by scheduling t on c. This process computes the state space of consistent schedulings that are also feasible for all $T' \in \mathcal{P}(T)$. This is an important property as it will allow us to extract schedulability properties simply by applying more filters on the resulted state space. The formal proof for this property is quite lengthy so we only sketch it here. All schedulings are consistent because we never schedule a task before the next available time of a core. As for the feasibility, we schedule a new task at each step as long as we respect its constraints, effectively computing all the schedulings for a larger subset of T than the schedulings we computed at the previous step.

```
1: A ← A₀
2: A' ← 0
3: while A' ≢ A do
4:     A' ← A
5:     for all ⟨t, c⟩ ∈ T × C do
6:         Φ ← fltrₜ(t) ∘ fltrₐ(𝒟(t)) ∘ fltrₑ(t, c)
7:         A ← A ∪ (sch(t, c) ∘ Φ)(A)
8:     end for
9: end while
```

Fig. 5. State space computation algorithm

Let us now describe the filter and scheduling operations as homomorphisms. Let $t \in T$ be a task and $c \in C$ be a core. We first define the filter that removes schedulings where t has already been scheduled:

$$fltr_t(t)(e, x) = \begin{cases} e \xrightarrow{x} id & \text{if } (e = t) \wedge (x = \epsilon) \\ e \xrightarrow{x} fltr_t(t) & \text{otherwise} \end{cases} \tag{1}$$

$$fltr_t(t)(1) = 0$$

Let $D = \mathcal{D}(t)$ be the dependencies of t. The filter that removes schedulings where the dependencies of t have not been executed yet is given by:

$$fltr_d(D)(e, x) = \begin{cases} e \xrightarrow{x} fltr_d(D - \{e\}) & \text{if } (e \in D) \wedge (x \neq \epsilon) \\ e \xrightarrow{x} fltr_d(D) & \text{otherwise} \end{cases}$$

$$fltr_d(D)(1) = \begin{cases} 0 & \text{if } D \neq \varnothing \\ 1 & \text{otherwise} \end{cases} \tag{2}$$

Let $ets(t, c, \tau) = \max(\tau, \mu_r(t))$ be a function that gives the time at which a task t is expected to start, if scheduled on a core c that is next available at time τ, Similarly Let $eta(t, c, \tau) = ets(t, c, \tau) + \mu_c(t)$ give the time at which a task is expected to finish. The filter that removes schedulings where the constraints of t cannot be satisfied on c is given by:

$$fltr_c(t, c)(e, x) = \begin{cases} e \xrightarrow{x} id & \text{if } (e = c) \wedge (eta(t, c, x) \leq \mu_d(t)) \\ e \xrightarrow{x} fltr_c(t, c) & \text{otherwise} \end{cases} \tag{3}$$

$$fltr_c(t, c)(1) = 0$$

Next, we define the homomorphism that schedules t on c, at its next available time. This must be split into two operations. The first takes care of the task scheduling, i.e. it updates the assignment of the task variable:

$$sch_\tau(t, c, \tau)(e, x) = \begin{cases} e \xrightarrow{c, \tau} id & \text{if } e = t \\ e \xrightarrow{x} sch_\tau(t, c, \tau) & \text{otherwise} \end{cases} \quad (4)$$

$$sch_\tau(t, c, \tau)(1) = 0$$

The second takes care of updating the next available time of the core, before it calls the second:

$$sch(t, c)(e, x) = \begin{cases} e \xrightarrow{eta(t, c, x)} sch_\tau(t, c, ets(t, c, x)) & \text{if } e = c \\ e \xrightarrow{x} sch(t, c) & \text{otherwise} \end{cases} \quad (5)$$

$$sch(t, c)(1) = 0$$

Finally, let $fltr(t, c) = fltr_t(t) \circ fltr_d(\mathcal{D}(t)) \circ fltr_c(t, c)$ be the composition of all filters, we can define the state space computation:

Definition 9. *Let $A_0 = c_1 \xrightarrow{0} c_2 \xrightarrow{0} \ldots t_1 \xrightarrow{\epsilon} t_2 \xrightarrow{\epsilon} \ldots 1$ be the DDD representing the singleton composed of a scheduling where no task is scheduled. Given a task model $\mathcal{M} = \langle T, \mu, \prec \rangle$, a set of cores $\mathcal{C}$ and the homomorphisms $fltr_t$, $fltr_d$, $fltr_c$ and sch, we can compute the state space of schedulings as the fixed point application of*

$$state\_space(\mathcal{M}, \mathcal{C}) = \left(id \cup \bigcup_{t \in T} \bigcup_{c \in \mathcal{C}} sch(t, c) \circ fltr(t, c) \right)^* \quad (6)$$

starting with A_0.

5.4   Dealing with Heterogeneous Cores

In the above, we have been assuming that it takes the same amount of time to execute the same task on any core. While this is a reasonable assumption for homogeneous multi-core architectures, it is not for heterogeneous ones, where some cores can be faster than others (e.g. ARM big.LITTLE [10]).

However, it is easy to adapt our state space computing technique to accommodate such architectures. Let $\gamma : \mathcal{C} \to \mathbb{R}$ be a function that assigns a scaling factor to each core, such that a task t will take $\lceil \mu_c(t)/\gamma(c) \rceil$ time units to run on c. Then, we simply need to modify the *eta* function such that:

$$eta(t, c, \tau) = ets(t, c, \tau) + \left\lceil \frac{\mu_c(t)}{\gamma(c)} \right\rceil$$

With that modification, *eta* takes into account the scaling factor of c, which in turn will reflect in the behaviours of $fltr_c$ and sch.

6   Schedulability Properties

Once we have computed the state space of schedulings for a given task model, we can extract various properties about its schedulability. We first describe how to extract the feasible (or k-relaxed feasible) and consistent schedulings from our state space, considering the optional failure of one or more cores. Then, we generalise this extraction process to the schedulings with arbitrary properties, such as a an upper bound on the time to complete all tasks.

6.1   Extracting Feasible Schedulings

Recalling Sect. 5, we know that given a set of tasks T and state space of schedulings A, the schedulability problem boils down to the existential quantification $\exists S \in A$ such that S is feasible and consistent for all tasks in T. In practice, if we built A with our *state_space* homomorphism, this can be carried out by the means of a filter on A that removes all paths where there is $t \in T$ that is not scheduled, i.e. it is assigned to ϵ. This is because all schedulings in A are consistent, and that applying such a filter would keep only those that are feasible for T. We can reuse the $fltr_d$ filter we defined in (2) to do that, applying it on the set of all tasks T.

Proposition 1. *Let $\mathcal{M} = \langle T, \mu, \prec \rangle$ be a task model and $\mathcal{C}$ a set of cores. Let $A = state\_space(\mathcal{M}, \mathcal{C})$ be the state space of schedulings. $\mathcal{M}$ is schedulable on $\mathcal{C}$ if and only if $fltr_d(T)(A) \not\equiv 0$.*

To model the failure of a particular core $c \in \mathcal{C}$, it suffices to further reduce the set of schedulings to those where c is not used. In order to do that, we can define a filter that works on the core variables, removing all the schedulings that use c beyond a certain point in time $\tau \in \mathbb{N}$. For the case of a purely static analysis, one could argue that the value of τ cannot be set as anything but 0, as it is not possible to guess *when* a core will fail. However, if we were to use a dynamic scheduler, we could make use of our state space to help our scheduler make an informed decision in the event of a core failure.

$$fltr_f(c, \tau)(e, x) = \begin{cases} e \xrightarrow{x} id & \text{if } (e = c) \wedge (x \leq \tau) \\ e \xrightarrow{x} fltr_f(c, \tau) & \text{otherwise} \end{cases} \qquad (7)$$

$$fltr_f(c, \tau)(1) = 0$$

Proposition 2. *If $A' = fltr_d(T)(A)$ represents the set of feasible and consistent schedulings for all tasks in T, then $fltr_f(c, \tau)(A') \subseteq A'$ is the subset of schedulings that tolerate the failure of $c \in \mathcal{C}$ after time $\tau \in \mathbb{N}$.*

Note that we could apply several instances of this homomorphism with different cores to model multiple core failures. Furthermore, the order in which we would apply any of our filters does not influence the result it will produce.

Similarly, k-relaxed schedulability can be deduced by the application of a series of filters on the state space of schedulings. In fact, we only need to slightly change our Proposition 1 to consider only the k-critical tasks.

Proposition 3. *Let* $\mathcal{M} = \langle T, \mu, \prec \rangle$ *be a task model and* $\mathcal{C}$ *a set of cores. Let* $A = $ *state_space*$(\mathcal{M}, \mathcal{C})$ *be the state space of schedulings.* $\mathcal{M}$ *is k-relaxed schedulable on* $\mathcal{C}$ *if and only if* $fltr_d(T_{\geq k})(A) \not\equiv 0$.

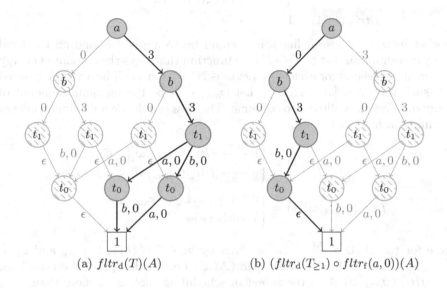

(a) $fltr_d(T)(A)$ (b) $(fltr_d(T_{\geq 1}) \circ fltr_f(a, 0))(A)$

Fig. 6. Two examples of schedulability verification.

Example 2. Let us illustrate our schedulability verification with a simple example. Let $T = \{t_0, t_1\}$ be a set of tasks, where $\mu(t_0) = \langle 0, 3, 4, 0 \rangle$ and $\mu(t_1) = \langle 0, 3, 4, 1 \rangle$. Let there be no dependencies between the tasks. Let $\mathcal{C} = \{a, b\}$ be a set of homogeneous cores. The DDDs of Fig. 6 depict the state space of schedulings $A = state\_space(\mathcal{M}, \mathcal{C})$. The left DDD shows the result of the application of $fltr_d$ for all tasks in T, where all removed nodes and arcs are greyed out. In other words, it reveals the two feasible and consistent schedulings in A; one with t_0 assigned on a at time 0 and t_1 assigned on b at time 0, and reversely. The right DDD shows the result of the composition of $fltr_d$ on all 1-critical tasks with $fltr_f$ on core a at time 0. In other words, it reveals the sole 1-relaxed feasible and consistent scheduling in A that tolerates the failure of the core a. This scheduling assigns t_1 on core b and ignores t_0.

6.2 Extracting Other Properties

We saw that extracting schedulings that respect some property such as the tolerance to a core failure amounts to applying an additional filter on the set of schedulings. Actually, we can generalise this approach to any kind of property. For instance, we could be interested in giving an upper bound on the total makespan of our schedulings, thus filtering out those that would exceed it. Such filter would be expressed as follows, with $\tau \in \mathbb{N}$ the upper bound:

$$fltr_{\mathrm{ms}}(\tau)(e, x) = \begin{cases} e \xrightarrow{\;x\;} 0 & \text{if } (e \in \mathcal{C}) \wedge (x > \tau) \\ e \xrightarrow{\;x\;} fltr_{\mathrm{ms}}(\tau) & \text{otherwise} \end{cases}$$

$$fltr_{\mathrm{ms}}(\tau)(1) = 1$$

Another interesting user-defined filter could be to apply a bound on the total energy consumption. Let $\zeta : \mathcal{C} \to \mathbb{N}$ be a function that gives the amount of energy consumed per second for each core. Let $\boldsymbol{\omega} \in \mathbb{N}^n$ with $n = |\mathcal{C}|$ be a vector indexed by $\mathcal{C}$ such that $\boldsymbol{\omega} = [\omega_{c_1}, \ldots, \omega_{c_n}]$. Let $\omega_{\max} \in \mathbb{N}$ be the maximum amount of energy our system is allowed to consume. Then we can define a maximum energy consumption filter as follows:

$$fltr_\omega(\omega_{\max}, \boldsymbol{\omega})(e, x) = \begin{cases} e \xrightarrow{\;c, \tau\;} fltr_\omega(\omega_{\max}, \boldsymbol{\omega}') & \text{if } e \in T \\ e \xrightarrow{\;x\;} fltr_\omega(\omega_{\max}, \boldsymbol{\omega}) & \text{otherwise} \end{cases}$$

$$fltr_\omega(\omega_{\max}, \boldsymbol{\omega})(1) = \begin{cases} 0 & \text{if } \sum_{c \in \mathcal{C}} \omega_c > \omega_{\max} \\ 1 & \text{otherwise} \end{cases}$$

where for the DDD $e \xrightarrow{\;c, \tau\;} d$, $\boldsymbol{\omega}'$ is given by $\forall c \in \mathcal{C} - \{e\}, \omega'_c = \omega_c$ and $\omega'_e = \omega_e + \zeta(c) \cdot \mu_c(t)$. Let $A = state\_space(\mathcal{M}, \mathcal{C})$ be a state space of schedulings, $A' = fltr_\omega(\omega_{\max}, \mathbf{0})(A)$ is the subset of schedulings not using more than $\omega_{\max}$ units of energy.

7   Experimental Results

We implemented our schedulability verification technique in C++ with libsdd (https://github.com/ahamez/libsdd), a generic library for decision diagrams. Our implementation is as close as possible to the approach we described in Sect. 5, with the exception of some minor optimizations. We used a task model generator that chooses task constraints and dependencies at random. We ran our tests for a 2-core and a 4-core architecture, with various number of tasks, on a 3.5 GHz Intel Xeon E5, with 64 GB memory and on a single thread.

Because we used random task models, we sometimes got broadly different results between executions, as the duration of the state space computation depends on the level of sharing the DDD can expose, which in turn depends on the constraints and dependencies of the tasks. We also noticed that the time to determine the non-schedulability of a task model was usually much smaller than the time to determine its schedulability. The reason is that our technique can quickly realise that there is no possible scheduling, after it tried to schedule all tasks at least once. When the system is schedulable, our method continues until it finished exploring all the possible schedulings, which can take significantly more time. So as to alleviate these discrepancies, for each number of tasks we averaged our result on a set of 10 model instances that were found schedulable. We aborted the runs that took more than 24 h. Our results are depicted in Fig. 7.

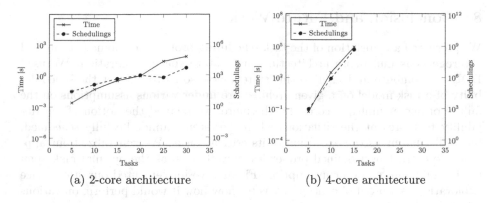

(a) 2-core architecture   (b) 4-core architecture

Fig. 7. Experimental results on tight models.

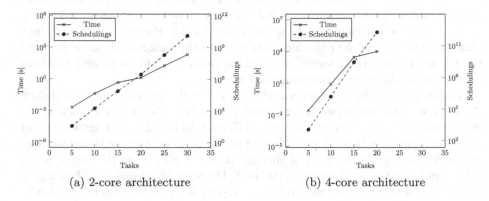

(a) 2-core architecture   (b) 4-core architecture

Fig. 8. Experimental results on loose models.

As we can see from those results, our technique does not scale well with the number of cores. The main reason for this is obviously the combinatorial explosion of the possible schedulings. It averaged at roughly 400 on a 2-core architecture for 15 tasks, while it was a million times more on a 4-core architecture. Furthermore, because of our variable ordering, adding more cores tends to create very wide DDDs. Indeed, we have to consider all possible times at which they will be next available, which is likely to create a lot of arcs just to represent all possible combination of cores utilisation.

Our task models used quite tight deadlines, so as to create hugely constrained problems. In order to see how our technique would perform with more loose models, we ran a second series of tests on a set of task models with very late deadlines. Our results are depicted in Fig. 8. As we can see, our method was able to compute fairly large state spaces but quickly failed to finish in a reasonable time on the 4-core architecture.

8 Conclusion and Future Works

We presented a translation of the task scheduling problem for homogeneous and heterogeneous multi-core architectures as a state space exploration. We used DDDs to compute and analyse this state space, so as to extract the schedulability of a task model on a given architecture under various assumptions on the failure of one or multiple cores. Furthermore, we relaxed the notion of schedulability to represent the situations where a system cannot be fully scheduled, but still guarantees the execution of its critical tasks. We generalized our approach to extract user-defined properties as well, such as the optimal makespan or the minimum energy consumption. Finally, we implemented our state space exploration as a proof of concept, so as to show how it would perform on various scheduling problems.

One axis of future work would be to handle transient errors. Defining a filter (i.e. a homomorphism) for that is not enough, as our state space exploration does not have a way to explicitly ignore a core for an arbitrary amount of time. One possibility would be to include *fake tasks* in the task model, so as to model the temporary failure of a core. A second approach would be to add arbitrary delays during the state space computation.

Another axis of future work would be to refine the encoding of a scheduling. As we saw from our experimental results, including the core variables in the representation tends to create very wide DDDs, which can have a negative effect on the computation time. A possible lead would be to anonymise those variables [8], so as to increase the level of sharing. It might also be worth investigating other kind of decision diagrams, such as Σ Decision Diagrams [9]. Similarly to what we achieved with homomorphisms, set-rewriting techniques might also be considered [14].

Finally, it could be interesting to abstract the notion of user-defined filter, so as to provide a schedulability analysis framework. One good abstraction would be the definition of a domain specific language that could express the the system and its constraints (the tasks) as well as the properties and possible failures to consider.

References

1. Baruah, S., Guo, Z.: Mixed-criticality scheduling upon varying-speed processors. In: 2013 IEEE 34th Real-Time Systems Symposium (RTSS), pp. 68–77. IEEE (2013)
2. Bryant, R.E.: Graph-based algorithms for boolean function manipulation. IEEE Trans. Comput. **C–35**(8), 677–691 (1986)
3. Burns, A., Davis, R.: Mixed criticality systems-a review. Department of Computer Science, University of York, Technical report (2013)
4. Cire, A.A., van Hoeve, W.J.: Multivalued decision diagrams for sequencing problems. Oper. Res. **61**(6), 1411–1428 (2013)
5. Cirinei, M., Bini, E., Lipari, G., Ferrari, A.: A flexible scheme for scheduling fault-tolerant real-time tasks on multiprocessors. In: 2007 IEEE International Parallel and Distributed Processing Symposium, pp. 1–8 (2007)

6. Clarke, E.M., Emerson, E.A., Sistla, A.P.: Automatic verification of finite-state concurrent systems using temporal logic specifications. ACM Trans. Program. Lang. Syst. **8**(2), 244–263 (1986)
7. Couvreur, J.-M., Encrenaz, E., Paviot-Adet, E., Poitrenaud, D., Wacrenier, P.-A.: Data decision diagrams for Petri Net analysis. In: Esparza, J., Lakos, C.A. (eds.) ICATPN 2002. LNCS, vol. 2360, pp. 101–120. Springer, Heidelberg (2002)
8. Hong, S., Kordon, F., Paviot-Adet, E., Evangelista, S.: Computing a hierarchical static order for decision diagram-based representation from P/T Nets. In: Jensen, K., Donatelli, S., Kleijn, J. (eds.) ToPNoC V. LNCS, vol. 6900, pp. 121–140. Springer, Heidelberg (2012)
9. Hostettler, S., Marechal, A., Linard, A., Risoldi, M., Buchs, D.: High-level petri net model checking with alpina. Fundam. Inform. **113**(3–4), 229–264 (2011). http://dx.doi.org/10.3233/FI-2011-608
10. Jeff, B.: Big. little system architecture from arm: saving power through heterogeneous multiprocessing and task context migration. In: Proceedings of the 49th Annual Design Automation Conference, pp. 1143–1146. ACM (2012)
11. Jensen, A.R., Lauritzen, L.B., Laursen, O.: Optimal task graph scheduling with binary decision diagrams (2004)
12. Kordon, F., Garavel, H., Hillah, L.M., Hulin-Hubard, F., Linard, A., Beccuti, M., Hamez, A., Lopez-Bobeda, E., Jezequel, L., Meijer, J., Paviot-Adet, E., Rodriguez, C., Rohr, C., Srba, J., Thierry-Mieg, Y., Wolf, K.: Complete Results for the 2015 Edition of theModel Checking Contest (2015). http://mcc.lip6.fr/2015/results.php
13. Linard, A., Paviot-Adet, E., Kordon, F., Buchs, D., Charron, S.: polydd: Towards a framework generalizing decision diagrams. In: 10th International Conference on Application of Concurrency to System Design, ACSD 2010, Braga, Portugal, 21–25 June 2010. pp. 124–133 (2010). http://dx.doi.org/10.1109/ACSD.2010.17
14. Lopez-Bobeda, E., Colange, M., Buchs, D.: Building a symbolic model checker from formal language description. In: 2015 15th International Conference on Application of Concurrency to System Design (ACSD), pp. 50–59 (2015)
15. Mushtaq, H., Al-Ars, Z., Bertels, K.: Survey of fault tolerance techniques for shared memory multicore/multiprocessor systems. In: 2011 IEEE 6th International Design and Test Workshop (IDT), pp. 12–17 (2011)
16. Nikolic, B., Bletsas, K., Petters, S.M.: Hard real-time multiprocessor scheduling resilient to core failures. In: 2015 IEEE 21st International Conference on Embedded and Real-Time Computing Systems and Applications, pp. 122–131 (2015)
17. Pathan, R.M.: Fault-tolerant real-time scheduling using chip multiprocessors. Proc. Suppl. vol. EDCC (2008)
18. Rice, M., Kulhari, S.: A survey of static variable ordering heuristics for efficient bdd/mdd construction. University of California, Technical report (2008)

Formal Verification of the On-the-Fly Vehicle Platooning Protocol

Piergiuseppe Mallozzi[1,2]([✉]), Massimo Sciancalepore[1,2],
and Patrizio Pelliccione[1,2]

[1] Chalmers University of Technology, Gothenburg, Sweden
mallozzi@chalmers.se, massimosciancalepore@gmail.com
[2] University of Gothenburg, Gothenburg, Sweden
patrizio.pelliccione@gu.se

Abstract. Future transportation systems are expected to be Systems of Systems (SoSs) composed of vehicles, pedestrians, roads, signs and other parts of the infrastructure. The boundaries of such systems change frequently and unpredictably and they have to cope with different degrees of uncertainty. At the same time, these systems are expected to function correctly and reliably. This is why designing for resilience is becoming extremely important for these systems.

One example of SoS collaboration is the vehicle platooning, a promising concept that will help us dealing with traffic congestion in the near future. Before deploying such scenarios on real roads, vehicles must be guaranteed to act safely, hence their behaviour must be verified. In this paper, we describe a vehicle platooning protocol focusing especially on dynamic leader negotiation and message propagation. We have represented the vehicles behaviours with timed automata so that we are able to formally verifying the correctness through the use of model checking.

1 Introduction

Intelligent and connected vehicles will be key elements of future of transportation systems. Within these systems, vehicles will act as standalone systems and at the same time they will interact each other as well as with pedestrians, roads, signs and other parts of the infrastructure to achieve (even temporarily) some common objectives. Future transportation systems might be then seen as Systems of Systems (SoSs) [10] in which the boundaries will change frequently and unpredictably. Moreover, these systems will need to cope with different degrees of uncertainty both at the level of single constituent systems and the entire SoS. Intelligent transport systems promise to solve issues related to road congestion, environment pollution and accidents for a better and more sustainable future [2]. In order to increase safety, reduce traffic congestion and enhance driving comfort, vehicles will cooperate exchanging information among each other and with the surrounding environment as well.

In this paper, we focus on a specific scenario, namely on-the-fly and opportunistic platooning, i.e. an unplanned platooning composed of cars that temporarily join in an ensemble to share part of their journey. Platooning is one

I. Crnkovic and E. Troubitsyna (Eds.): SERENE 2016, LNCS 9823, pp. 62–75, 2016.
DOI: 10.1007/978-3-319-45892-2_5

of the promising concepts to help us dealing with traffic jams and at the same time to increase the overall safety while driving. A platoon consists of reducing the distances among following vehicles; it consists of a *leading* vehicle driving manually and one or more *following* vehicles automatically driving and following the leader one after another. This concept has been studied and applied especially in trucks for the transportation of goods [1] with the aim of reducing the impact with air and consume less fuel, but not as much work has been done regarding normal vehicles platooning. Each vehicle must be able to communicate with the others, or at least with the cars adjacent in the platoon. The communication is important because each vehicle needs to adjust the speed and the distance according to the other vehicles information. Also, the leader of the platoon is responsible for managing the overall platoon formation, by accepting new vehicles or responding to vehicles leaving.

Platooning is also a way towards autonomous vehicles since, except for the leader, the vehicles do not need human intervention during the travel journey. Since human intervention is no longer needed, all decisions must be taken autonomously by the vehicle, and this is a huge challenge for safety assurance. Consequently, on the one side the use of platooning promises to enhance safety, and on the other side safety is exposed to new threats and challenges. It is important to notice that nowadays most of the systems are guaranteed to operate correctly only in certain configurations and within the system boundaries. When these boundaries are removed and the system is exposed to unpredictable and uncontrollable scenarios and environments, safety guarantees no longer hold. This will be one of the greatest challenges of future autonomous and connected vehicles that will cooperate with other vehicles, pedestrians, roads, etc. in a SoS setting.

Although there are different levels of autonomy of vehicles[1], autonomous vehicles can be considered as particular self-adaptive systems [4] since they are capable of adapting themselves at runtime. A connected vehicle beside being self-adaptive is also open to interactions with other vehicles and other elements of the external environment. The unpredictability and uncontrollably of the environment hamper the complete understanding of the system at design time. Often uncertainty is resolved only at runtime when vehicles will face with concrete and specific instantiations of the pre-defined environment parameters. This implies that the certification process for safety has to be extended also to runtime phases.

In this paper, we focus on a platooning scenario where the different vehicle's behaviours are organized in various modes [16]. A mode is a concept for structuring the overall behaviour of the system into a set of different behaviours, each of them activated at different times according to specific circumstances. The behaviour of each mode is then represented in terms of a state machine that captures the behaviour of the system in a specific modality, e.g. during the

---

[1] The National Highway Traffic Safety Administration (NHTSA) has proposed a formal classification system based on five levels: "*U.S. Department of Transportation Releases Policy on Automated Vehicle Development. National Highway Traffic Safety Administration, 2013*".

selection of a leader of the platoon, leaving a platoon, etc. Transitions among states can be triggered by timing constraints or external events. A special transition can lead the system to a different mode: in this case the two states involved are *border states* of the modes. Figure 1 shows a vehicle platooning scenario that involves different heterogeneous vehicles. Each vehicle is in a certain mode according to its behaviour; we will describe the modes in more detail later. The communication among the vehicles is represented with dotted blue lines.

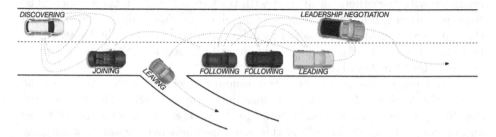

Fig. 1. Dynamic vehicle platooning scenarios. Each vehicle is in a certain mode according to its behaviour in the platoon. (Color figure online)

In this paper, we formally verify the on-the-fly vehicle platooning protocol through the use of the Uppaal [6] model checker. More precisely we verify the absence of deadlocks in the mode-switching protocol as well as other interesting properties.

The rest of the paper is structured as follows: Sect. 2 presents all the modes of our platooning scenario, Sect. 3 describes some parts of the Uppaal model, and Sect. 4 describes the properties we checked on our model. In Sect. 5 we show the results of a concrete simulation of our model in Uppal. Section 6 presents the results of the validation we performed through the use of the model checker Uppaal. Section 7 discusses works that are related to our work and finally Sect. 8 concludes the paper with directions for our future work.

2   Multi-mode System

Partitioning a system into multiple modes, each of which describing a specific behaviour of the system, is a common approach in system design. It leads to a series of advantages, such as reducing the software complexity and easing the addition of new features [16]. A self-adaptive system can be considered as a multimode system; if something happens in the environment, the system switches mode in order to adapt to the new conditions. This is the design strategy we follow in this paper.

We start by partitioning our system into different operational modes, recognizing different system behaviours. We have defined the different modes as a set of connected states with common behaviours. There are particular states that we call *border states*: to pass from one mode to another, the system passes through these states. All the modes have one or more *border states* that allow the mode switching of the system. Switching from one mode to another means that the system is passing from one border state of the current mode to a border state of another mode. For each vehicle taking part in the platoon we have identified the following modes:

- *Discovering*: this is the entering mode of the vehicle that wants to take part in a platoon and searches for other vehicles that have the same goals (e.g. common destination).
- *Forming*: the first two vehicles that want to form a new platoon enter into this mode. To do that, they decide who will be the leading vehicle of the platoon.
- *Joining*: a vehicle has found an existing platoon and it wants to join it. The vehicle can be accepted in the platoon within a certain time interval;
- *Leading*: the vehicle with the best safety attributes is elected as leader of the platoon. We have assumed that each vehicle shares its safety attributes with the other vehicles. Once in this mode, the vehicle has to steer the following vehicles, propagate information, keep track of the list of the followers, accept new vehicles that want to join, and, finally, manage the leaving of the followers.
- *Following*: all the vehicles drive in automated manner and follow the leader. A follower can receive information from the leader and propagate it to the other members of the platoon. It also supports the changing of the leader and if the leader leaves then the vehicle goes into the discovering mode again.
- *Leaving*: all the vehicles can leave the platoon at arbitrary time. When the leader leaves, the platoon dissolves. When a follower leaves, it must advise the leader and receive acknowledgement.
- *Dissolving*: vehicle goes in the dissolving mode when (i) it is a follower and does not have a leader anymore or (ii) it is a leader and does not have followers anymore. From this mode, it can either leave or go back to the discovering mode and start a new platoon.
- *Negotiation*: when a new vehicle wants to take part of an existing platoon, either it becomes a follower or it has to negotiate the leadership with the current leader. The vehicle with the highest safety attributes will always be the leader. Leadership negotiation can also be triggered by two platoons that want to merge.

3   Uppaal Model Description

Our strategy to model the behaviour of the on-the-fly platooning is to build a generic Uppaal template that incorporates all the modes. This template can be then instantiated for each vehicle that will take part to a specific scenario. More precisely, this model can be instantiated by all the vehicles regardless of their role in the platoon. We can then simulate a variety of scenarios by tuning the

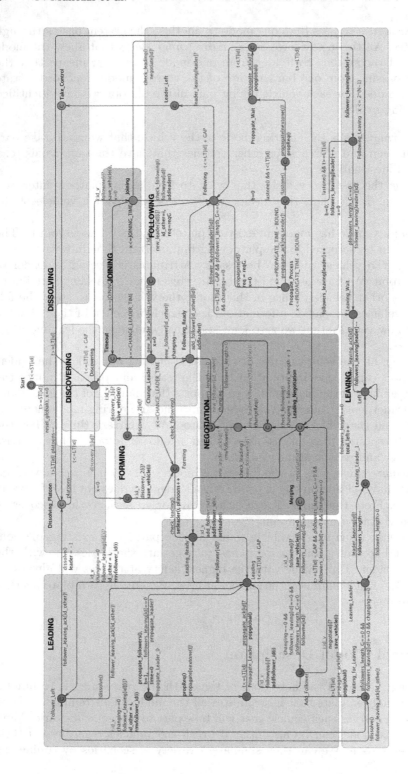

Fig. 2. Uppaal model with modes.

vehicles intrinsic properties. This solution is more scalable than having multiple models for different roles of the platoon (leader, follower) (Fig. 2).

The dynamic leader negotiation is a property of our scenario since we do not know who is going to be the leader beforehand. Furthermore, the leader can be changed during the platoon life. In order to this, we assume that each vehicle has associated a parameter representing its safety characteristics, called safety index, before it enters the platoon. Our models and protocol assure that the leader is always the vehicle with the highest safety index. The safety index it is just a value and it represents the overall safety score of the vehicle, the higher the better. We can assume that this value is calculated taking into consideration all safety-related parameters of the vehicle, either static ones such as the year of the vehicle, the size or dynamic ones taking into consideration the driver experience and the people on board.

In our model every vehicle starts from a *discovering* mode where it looks for other vehicles or platoons to join. In fact, the *formation* of a platoon can happen in different ways:

- Two vehicles negotiating with each other and forming one platoon with one leader and one follower. The two vehicles negotiate the leadership according to their safety index.
- One vehicle joining an existing platoon if there is already a formed platoon and the new vehicle is in discovery mode.
- Two existing platoons merging into one after the two leaders have performed a re-negotiation of their leadership.

If the joining of a platoon takes more than the pre-defined constant time (JOINING_TIME) to a vehicle, then it goes into discovering mode again. After the formation phase a vehicle can be either in *Leaving* or in *Following* state. The leader keeps track of all its followers at any time by listening to new joining or leaving requests. It can also send messages to all its followers. Message propagation can happen in two ways:

- The leader can reach all its followers and communicate with them all.
- The leader sends a message to the follower immediately behind him and then the message will propagate from follower to follower until reaching the last vehicle in the platoon.

We also take into consideration the propagation time that is needed for a vehicle to pass on the message to the next vehicle. The time is, in fact, crucial for safety-related messages; we want to be sure that the message reaches the whole platoon in the shortest time. We guarantee this by formulating and verifying time-related properties on the message propagation as described in the section below. Another feature of our model is the dynamic leader negotiation also after the platoon has been formed. This can happen in two cases:

- Two platoons want to merge. The platoon with the leader having the highest safety index will take the leadership while the other leader activates the joining procedure to the new leader that has to be completed in CHANGE_LEADER_ TIME and afterward it becomes a follower of the newly elected leader.

- A vehicle wants to join an existing platoon and it has a safety index higher than the platoon leader. The current leader passes its followers to the new leader and itself becomes a follower.

4 Requirement Specifications Verified with Model Checking

The main purpose of a model-checker is to verify the model with respect to a requirement specification. With the timed-automata representation of the system, it is possible to verify safety and behavioural properties of our model such as the absence of deadlocks or the propagation of a safety-critical message within a certain time. Like the model, the requirement specification (or properties) to be checked must be expressed in a formally well-defined and machine readable language. Uppaal utilizes a subset of TCTL (timed computation tree logic) [3,7]. The path formulae $A <> \varphi$ (or equivalently $A <> \varphi = \neg E[\,]\neg\varphi$) expresses that φ will be eventually satisfied or more precisely that in each path will exist a state that satisfies φ. The path formulae $A[\,]\varphi$ expresses that φ should be true in all reachable states.

In order to verify the safety requirements, we have to build a scenario first, i.e., a particular instantiation of the system. Our model is made in order to be configured according to the scenario we want to verify. We first need to set the *number of vehicles* involved and for each vehicle we need to configure few parameters such as its *arrival time*, *leaving time*, and *safety index*. We have automated the configuration process by assigning random values to these values as we explain in the following section. The automation process involves also the properties that are tuned according to the scenario we want to verify. Once we have configured our scenario we can formally verify the following properties:

- *Property 1: If a vehicle is in the leading mode then its safety index is higher then all other vehicles involved in the platoon.*
  Assuming a scenario where Vehicle 3 has the highest safety index the instantiated property would be expressed as:

$$A[] \ (\text{Vehicle}(3).\text{Leading} \implies \forall(i:id\_v) \ S[3] >= S[i])$$

- *Property 2: The propagation of a message from the leader to the last follower happens in a bounded amount of time.*
  The time in which the propagation has to happen varies according to the size of the platoon and the maximum acceptable delay is kept by the predefined variable MAX_PROP_DELAY.

$$A[](b==1 \implies time <= MAX\_PROP\_DELAY)$$

A boolean variable b and a clock variable *time* are two global variables that are used to measure the propagation time from when a message is fired. In order to measure that, when a message starts propagating, the variable b is set to 1 while time is reset. The properties assures that time will always be inferior to the constant MAX_PROP_DELAY while b is kept to 1. The variable b will be reset when the message has reached the last follower of the platoon.

- *Property 3: For each vehicle in the following state exists at least one vehicle in leading mode.*

$$A[] (\forall(k:id\_v) \ Vehicle(k).Following \implies$$
$$\exists \ (i:id\_v) \ Vehicle(i).All\_Leading\_States)$$

Since the leading mode is formed by a series of states this property is verified by including all the states of the leading mode (as a series of or elements). We did not write the full property for readability purposes.

- *Property 4: Whenever the vehicle with the highest safety index starts participating in the platooning it will eventually become the leader.*
Assuming that Vehicle 1 is the one with the highest safety index, the property becomes:

$$Vehicle(1).Start \implies <> Vehicle(1).Leading$$

- *Property 5: For all the path, the vehicle with the highest safety index goes into the leading state.*
Assuming the Vehicle 1 is the one with the highest safety index, the property becomes:

$$A<> Vehicle(1).Leading$$

- *Property 6: All vehicles will eventually leave the platoon.*
Since all the vehicles have a leaving time we can verify that:

$$A<> (\forall(i:id\_v) \ Vehicle(i).Start \implies$$
$$\forall(k:id\_v)Vehicle(k).Left)$$

- *Property 7: If a leader leaves the platoon then all its followers leave as well.*

$$A[] ((\exists(i:id\_v) \ Vehicle(i).Leaving\_Leader \land$$
$$\forall(k:id\_v) \ Vehicle(k).Following) \implies$$
$$\forall(j:id\_v) \ Vehicle(j).Dissolving\_Platoon)$$

- *Property 8: The model is deadlock free.*
Finally, this property assures that for all possible paths there are no deadlocks in our model:

$$A[] \neg deadlock$$

In Sect. 6 we present the verification times of the properties described above. We have noticed that properties apparently very similar require a very different amount of processing time in order to be verified. For example, both properties 4 and 5 verify the leadership of the vehicle with the highest safety index. Property 5 is always verified in less than 1 second, with the time increasing linearly with the number of vehicles. Property 4, instead, can take up to hundreds of seconds with an exponential increase with respect to the number of vehicles.

5 Simulation

Latest versions of Uppaal offer the possibility to perform a concrete simulation of the model. It is a verification tool that enables examination of the dynamic executions of a system. The simulation is based on concrete traces, e.g., one can choose a specific time to fire a transition. The tool helps to see at which time a transition can be fired. We have modeled some transition to fire with a uniform probability distribution. For example, in the propagation of the message, the transition will fire somewhere between PROPAGATE_TIME−BOUND and PROPAGATE_TIME+BOUND time units. We have used these time constraints to verify time properties based on the worst case scenarios when a message has to be propagated from the leader throughout the entire platoon.

In order to perform a simulation, we have to configure our model specifying parameters such as the number of vehicles, starting times, leaving times, and safety indexes. Each vehicle is an instance of the general vehicle template and by launching the simulation we can see how the vehicles interact with each other. All instances start from the same state and as the time flows Uppaal randomly selects which edge to fire among the available ones of each state. Some edges have guards and invariant in order to model the time of the transition from one state to another as a uniform probability distribution.

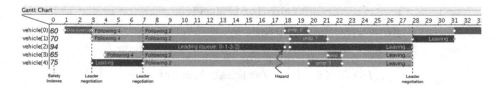

Fig. 3. Concrete simulation with Gantt Chart in Uppaal. (Color figure online)

Figure 3 shows the Gantt chart of a simulation. The horizontal axis represents the time span and in the vertical axis the list of vehicles instantiated in the simulation. A vertical line is used to represent the current time (which corresponds to the one displayed in the Simulation Trace-combo box). Horizontal bars of varying lengths and colours represent the different modes of the vehicles. Due to the limited amount of colours we are only able to show a limited amount of modes, specifically: discovering (purple), leading (blue), and following modes (green).

In the simulation showed in Fig. 3 we can see 5 vehicles participating in the platooning, each with a different safety index. vehicle0 starts first stays in the discovering mode until other vehicles enter in the platoon. When vehicle1 and vehicle4 enter, the three vehicles perform a leader negotiation and vehicle4 goes starts leading the platoon since it has the highest index. At time 4 vehicle3 joins the existing platoon until vehicle2 comes into play and renegotiate the leadership with vehicle4 and so on. It is also interesting to see the message propagation of a hazard from the leader to all its following vehicles (marked in red).

6   Verification Results

The simulation shown in Fig. 3 refers exclusively to a particular scenario. In this section, we instead report the results of an exhaustive verification that we performed on a number of different scenarios. This is obtained by automating the verification process with an external script that is able to generate different scenarios by changing the *number of vehicles* involved in the platoon and by randomly selecting independent variables within each vehicle, such as:

- *Arrival time*: the arrival time of a vehicle;
- *Leaving time*: the leaving time of a vehicle;
- *Safety index*: the safety index of a vehicle.

We are then able to verify all the properties described in Sect. 4 with a number of vehicles from 2 to 5 and for each vehicle configuration we run 100 tests with random scenarios. The height properties are verified by each generated configuration.

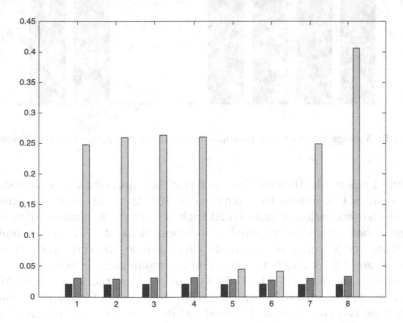

Fig. 4. Average verification times for 100 iterations. X-axes represent the property being verified. Y-axes the time to verifying it (in seconds). 2-3-4 vehicles scenario respectively

The script generates different models of the system based on a progressive number of the vehicles N and random values of some attributes. It executes two big loops, one to change the random values and one to increment the number of vehicles N. Thanks to the standalone Uppaal verifier, the script verifies the above-mentioned properties with random attribute values of all the models generated. If one property is not satisfied, the standalone verifier generates the counterexample, which is useful to understand why the property is not satisfied. Counterexample files can be open within the GUI of Uppaal. In the end, the script generates a report of the verification, i.e., a text file that traces all the properties, both if they are satisfied or not.

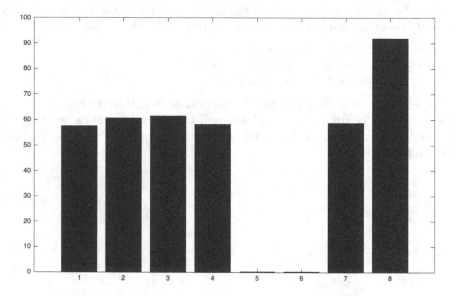

Fig. 5. Average times of 100 iterations for verifying the properties 5 vehicles

Figure 4 reports the time required to verify the 8 properties. The time shown in the figure is the average time required in 100 iterations. Since the time to complete the verification is exponential with respect to the number of vehicles the figure shows the time required by configurations of 2, 3, and 4 vehicles for verifying the 8 properties. For readability purpose, the verification time for configurations of 5 vehicles is not shown in the figure and the average times for 100 iterations are shown in Fig. 5. As we can see from the figure properties 5 and 6 have times comparable with the verifications times of 2, 3 and 4 vehicles. In fact, these two properties scale linearly while the others scale exponentially.

We have seen how changing the number of vehicles affects the verification time although these change a lot also for every configuration taken into consideration. Within the same number of vehicles, we have performed 100 iterations assigning random values to the vehicle attributes. Figure 6 shows how the verification time of a single property with a 5 vehicles configuration is affected by the random assignment of the vehicle attributes.

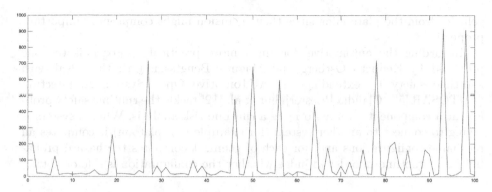

Fig. 6. Verification times of the deadlock free property for 5 vehicles scenario in 100 iterations.

7 Related Works

Kamali et al. [9] have also investigated the verification of vehicle platooning representing it as a multi-agents system. They verified the behaviour partly on the actual agent code and partly with Uppaal with timed-automata abstractions by using two different models, one for the follower and one for the leader.

One of the main challenges in open and self-adaptive systems is to certify that the system is always in a safe state. Since safety cannot be completely evaluated and assured at design time, at least part of the safety assurance must be shifted at run-time. The first ideas for certifying safety at runtime were introduced by Rushby [13,14]. He proposes an initial idea to certification based on formal analysis at runtime; however much work must be done to produce a solution that can be used concretely.

A promising approach to deal with safety certification at runtime is Con-Sert [15]. ConSert introduces the idea of *Conditional Safety Certificates* to facilitate the certification of open adaptive systems. Each subsystem is certified by a modular safety certificate based on a contract-like approach. The evaluation and the composition of the modular certificates happen at runtime. This framework offers flexibility as allows designers to specify safety through variable safety-certificates. Within the approach, all the configurations that a component of the system can assume must be predefined at design time in order to be certified "safe" at runtime. It allows emergent adaptive behaviours only if they can be tamed in certain boundaries with the concept of safety cages. Fully emergent behaviours are not possible to certify with ConSert hence ensuring safety in these cases is a much more difficult problem. A possible research direction can be investigating the theoretical assume-guarantee framework proposed in [8]. This framework allows one to efficiently define under which conditions adaptation can be performed by still preserving desired properties. The framework might provide the infrastructure to automatically calculate at runtime which properties are verified in specific scenarios. For instance, this might suggest excluding some vehicles from the platooning since their inclusion might compromise important properties.

Regarding the automotive domain a more practical approach is the one proposed by Kenneth Östberg and Magnus Bengtsson [11]; they deal with run-time safety by extending the AUTomotive Open System Architecture (AUTOSAR [5]). Claudia Priesterjahnr et al. [12] tackle the runtime safety problem at a component level performing a runtime risk analysis. When a system is trying to connect to another system (for example in a platoon) it computes all reachable configurations and, for each of them, it computes the hazard probabilities at runtime in order to judge whether the configuration is safe or not.

8   Conclusion

In this paper, we have presented the formal verification of on-the-fly vehicle platooning. We have modeled the vehicle behaviours with timed-automata so that we were able to verify the correctness of the protocol with model checking. We were able to verify that some properties always hold for a different number of vehicles each with random attributes. All the vehicles are modeled with a unique generic Uppaal model that can be instantiated for each specific vehicle. In this way, it is possible to simulate different scenarios and the verification is easily scalable to more vehicles. Each scenario has been generated with a script, which changes parameters such as the number of vehicles and the attributes for each vehicle and then it verifies that all the properties hold. We have focused our attention only to some interesting part of the model such as the dynamic leader negotiation and the message propagation of the vehicles leaving other parts to be further exploited. As future work, we plan to refine our model by releasing some assumptions made during the creation of the model and verifying more properties. As a long term goal, we plan to experiment with the protocol by using a set of miniature vehicles.

Acknowledgement. This work was partially supported by the NGEA Vinnovaproject and by the Wallenberg Autonomous Systems Program(WASP).

References

1. Current State of EU Legislation - Cooperative Dynamic Formation of Platoons for Safe and Energy-optimized Goods Transportation. http://www.companion-project.eu/wp-content/uploads/COMPANION-D2.2-Current-state-of-the-EU-legislation.pdf
2. Intelligent transport systems - Innovating for the transport of the future. http://ec.europa.eu/transport/themes/its/index_en.htm
3. Alur, R., Courcoubetis, C., Dill, D.: Model-checking for real-time systems. In: Proceedings of the Fifth Annual IEEE Symposium on Logic in Computer Science, LICS 1990, pp. 414–425. IEEE (1990)
4. de Lemos, R., et al.: Software engineering for self-adaptive systems: a second research roadmap. In: Lemos, R., Giese, H., Müller, H.A., Shaw, M. (eds.) Self-Adaptive Systems. LNCS, vol. 7475, pp. 1–32. Springer, Heidelberg (2013)

5. Fürst, S., Mössinger, J., Bunzel, S., Weber, T., Kirschke-Biller, F., Heitkämper, P., Kinkelin, G., Nishikawa, K., Lange, K.: Autosar-a worldwide standard is on the road. In: 14th International VDI Congress Electronic Systems for Vehicles, Baden-Baden, vol. 62 (2009)
6. David, A., Behrmann, G., Larsen, K.G.: A tutorial on uppaal 4.0, 28 November 2006
7. Henzinger, T.A., Nicollin, X., Sifakis, J., Yovine, S.: Symbolic model checking for real-time systems. Inf. Comput. **111**(2), 193–244 (1994)
8. Inverardi, P., Pelliccione, P., Tivoli, M.: Towards an assume-guarantee theory for adaptable systems. In: Proceedings of the ICSE Workshop on Software Engineering for Adaptive and Self-Managing Systems, SEAMS 2009, pp. 106–115. IEEE Computer Society, Washington, DC (2009)
9. McAree, O., Fisher, M., Kamali, M., Dennis, L.A., Veres, S.M.: Formal verification of autonomous vehicle platooning, 5 February 2016
10. Nielsen, C.B., Larsen, P.G., Fitzgerald, J., Woodcock, J., Peleska, J.: Systems of systems engineering: basic concepts, model-based techniques, and research directions. ACM Comput. Surv. **48**(2), 18:1–18:41, September 2015
11. Östberg, K., Bengtsson, M.: Run time safety analysis for automotive systems in an open and adaptive environment. In: SAFECOMP 2013-Workshop, NA, September 2013
12. Priesterjahnr, C.: Runtime safety analysis for safe reconfiguration, pp. 1–6, June 2013
13. Rushby, J.: Just-in-time certification. In: 12th IEEE International Conference on Engineering Complex Computer Systems, pp. 15–24. IEEE (2007)
14. Rushby, J.: Runtime certification. In: Leucker, M. (ed.) RV 2008. LNCS, vol. 5289, pp. 21–35. Springer, Heidelberg (2008)
15. Schneider, D., Trapp, M.: Conditional safety certification of open adaptive systems. ACM Trans. Auton. Adapt. Syst. **8**(2), 1–20 (2013)
16. Hansson, H., Hang, Y., Carlson, J.: Towards mode switch handling in component-based multi-mode systems. In: Proceedings of 15th International ACM SIGSOFT Symposium on Component Based Software Engineering, CBSE 2012, Bertinoro, Italy, pp. 183–188, June 2012

Engineering Resilient Systems

WRAD: Tool Support for Workflow Resiliency Analysis and Design

John C. Mace[✉], Charles Morisset, and Aad van Moorsel

School of Computing Science, Newcastle University,
Newcastle upon Tyne NE1 7RU, UK
{john.mace,charles.morisset,aad.vanmoorsel}@ncl.ac.uk

Abstract. Designing efficient workflows is complex especially when considering security constraints that restrict which users can perform which tasks. This is further exacerbated when considering users could become unavailable at runtime, which is known as the workflow resiliency problem. Ideally, designers undertake resiliency analysis at the design stage so that the likely impact of security constraints on a workflow can be assessed before its execution. In this paper, we describe a new tool called *Workflow Resiliency Analysis and Design* (WRAD) which automatically encodes a textual description of a workflow into the probabilistic model-checker PRISM, and carries out a resiliency evaluation. WRAD also computes optimal change sets for security constraints to assure a given resiliency threshold is reached.

Keywords: Workflow satisfiability problem · Probabilistic model checker · User availability

1 Introduction

Workflow is a concept used widely by business to formally represent and automatically manage day to day business processes [3]. Designing a workflow generally consists of two main design elements. The first is a *workflow specification*, which captures the business process structure in terms of tasks (the work) and the order (the flow) in which tasks should be performed to reach the business goal. The second design element is a *workflow security policy* containing constraints restricting which users can perform which tasks in each workflow execution.

Productivity and security are often a source of tension as one commonly impacts the other [10]. Productivity may be impacted even further when considering users may become unavailable at runtime (e.g., sickness, vacation, other tasks) and the security constraints prohibit all users who remain available from completing the workflow. A measure of workflow productivity assuming possible user unavailability is *workflow resiliency*, defined as the maximum probability of finding a complete and valid *plan*, that is an assignment of users to tasks such that all tasks are assigned and all constraints are satisfied [6].

© Springer International Publishing Switzerland 2016
I. Crnkovic and E. Troubitsyna (Eds.): SERENE 2016, LNCS 9823, pp. 79–87, 2016.
DOI: 10.1007/978-3-319-45892-2_6

Workflow resiliency analysis can help workflow and security policy designers understand the impact of their design elements on workflow completion. Such analysis at the design stage could help avoid the (costly) need for policy redesign after a workflow is found unworkable. Computing the resiliency of a workflow requires a designer to establish the existence of a plan, a problem shown in general to be NP hard even before considering user unavailability, meaning all possible combinations of users to tasks may need to be tried [11].

To overcome this complexity we present a new tool called *Workflow Resiliency Analysis and Design* (WRAD), which helps workflow and security policy designers predict how resiliency is impacted by changes in a workflow. In [6] we showed that resiliency could be computed by solving a Markov decision process encoding the assignment process of a workflow. WRAD incorporates this approach by automatically encoding an inputted textual workflow description into the probabilistic model checker PRISM which provides an efficient way to solve Markov decision processes [5]. WRAD then evaluates and outputs the resiliency of the workflow.

If the resiliency is insufficient, the security policy designer may need to change security constraints. WRAD computes optimal 'change sets' for three types of security constraints that can be added or removed in order to reach a required resiliency threshold, and evaluates the expected resiliency for each change set. Once all optimal change sets have been found, the designer may choose which one(s) to implement, for instance in order to reach a satisfactory productivity-security trade-off. Section 2 describes some formal background on workflow resiliency, Sect. 3 gives an overview of our tool WRAD, and Sect. 4 contains related work and concluding remarks.

2   Workflow Fundamentals

In this section we give formal background of workflow and workflow resiliency.

Definition 1. *A workflow is a tuple $W = ((T, \prec), U, (A, S, B))$ where its specification is the partially ordered set of tasks $(T, \prec)$, users the set U, and security policy the tuple of relations (A, S, B).*

Each pair $(t, t') \in \prec$ indicates a sequential flow of tasks where t must be performed before t' in every instance of the workflow. A parallel flow of tasks is indicated if $t \nprec t'$ and $t' \nprec t$ such that t and t' may be performed in either order and we assume this choice on ordering to be non-deterministic. The relation $A \subseteq T \times U$ denotes authorisation constraints such that $(t, u) \in A$ indicates user u is authorised to be assigned to task t. The relation $S \subseteq T \times T$ denotes separation of duty constraints where for any $(t, t') \in T$, different users must be assigned to t and t', and $B \subseteq T \times T$ denotes binding of duty constraints where for any $(t, t') \in B$, the same user must be assigned to t and t'.

Definition 2. *Given a workflow $W = ((T, \prec), U, (A, S, B))$ and availability configuration θ, workflow resiliency is the maximum probability of finding a complete and valid plan.*

A *plan* specifies a runtime assignment of users to workflow tasks, represented as a relation $P \subseteq T \times U$, such that $(t, u) \in P$ indicates user u assigned to task t. A plan P is *complete* if it contains a user assignment for all tasks, otherwise P is *partial*. A plan P is *valid* in respect to a workflow W if it satisfies all constraints in the workflow's security policy (A, S, B). One approach to finding a plan is to select and assign each 'ready' task t to a valid and available user u. All previous assignments are defined as a valid partial plan P meaning t is deemed 'ready' only if all tasks t' ordered before t have already been assigned, in other words there exists an assignment $(t', u') \in P$. User u is valid if $P \cup \{(t, u)\}$ is also a valid partial plan. Ready tasks are selected and assigned until either a complete and valid plan is found, or a task is selected for which no users are valid or all valid users are unavailable, meaning no such plan exists.

User availability in workflow is a complex notion and we discuss different ways this may be modelled in [8]. We abstract the notion of availability as an *availability configuration* function $\theta : \mathbb{N} \times U \rightarrow [0, 1]$ which given the number of assigned tasks $0 \leq \mathbb{N} \leq (|T| - 1)$ and a user u returns the probability of u being available after $\mathbb{N}$ tasks have been assigned and executed. The number of assigned tasks at any point in a workflow instance is equivalent to the number of assignments defined in the current valid partial plan, that is $\mathbb{N} = |P|$. We encapsulate workflow resiliency as a function $\delta : W \times \theta \rightarrow [0, 1]$ which given a workflow W and an availability configuration θ returns a resiliency value between 0 and 1, where 1 indicates a plan will always be found whilst 0 indicates a plan will never be found. Note the security constraints we consider are independent of task order when finding a valid plan. However, we still consider task order in Definition 1 as it can have an impact on the resiliency of a workflow.

3   WRAD

In this section we introduce our new tool *Workflow Resiliency Analysis and Design* (WRAD), define the optimal constraints problem, and describe the process WRAD undertakes to evaluate the resiliency of a workflow and all optimal changes to the three types of security constraint we consider. An overview of WRAD's main components is also given.

Optimal Constraints Problem. WRAD provides security policy designers with optimised changes to security constraints, which ensure a minimum resiliency threshold is reached. WRAD automatically generates all such changes by solving the optimal constraints problem.

Definition 3. *Given a workflow* $W = ((T, \prec), U, (A, S, B))$, *availability configuration* θ, *a size bound* q, *and resiliency threshold* r, *the optimal constraints problem consists of finding all feasible and optimal change sets.*

A *change set* C_X is a set of security constraints that can be added ($C_A \rightarrow$ authorisations) or removed ($C_S \rightarrow$ separations, or $C_B \rightarrow$ bindings) to a workflow

Algorithm 1. Optimal changes to authorisation constraints where $\mathbb{C}_A$ is the set of all optimal change sets

---

1: **Inputs:**
      $W = ((T, \prec), U, (A, S, B)),\ \theta,\ \delta,\ q,\ r$
2: **Initialize:**
      $\mathbb{C}_A = \emptyset,\ V = \emptyset$
3: **if** $\delta(W, \theta) \geq r$ **then return** $\mathbb{C}_A$
4: **else** $V = \{(t, u) \mid t \in T, u \in U\}$
5:     **if** $\delta(((T, \prec), U, (V, S, B)), \theta) < r$ **then return** $\mathbb{C}_A$
6:     **else**
7:         **for** $i = 1 \rightarrow q$ **do**
8:             $\mathbb{F} = \{|F| = i \mid F \in \mathcal{P}(V \setminus A)\}$
9:             **if** $\mathbb{F} = \emptyset$ **then** *break*
10:           **else**
11:               **for** $F \in \mathbb{F}$ **do**
12:                 **if** $\delta(((T, \prec), U, (A \cup F, S, B)), \theta) \geq r$ **then**
13:                     $\mathbb{C}_A \cup \{F\}$
14:                     $V = V \setminus F$
15:         **return** $\mathbb{C}_A$

W, and we write $W \pm C_X$ to denote such a change. A change set C_X is feasible iff:

$$|C_X| \leq q,\ \delta(W \pm C_X, \theta) \geq r$$

Where q is a size bound indicating the maximum number of constraints allowed in each change set and r is a minimum resiliency threshold between 0 and 1. A change set C_X is considered optimal iff:

$$\nexists C'_X \subset C_X,\ \delta(W \pm C'_X, \theta) \geq r$$

We write $\mathbb{C}_A$, $\mathbb{C}_S$, and $\mathbb{C}_B$ for the respective sets of feasible and optimal change sets for authorisation, separation and binding constraints. Algorithm 1 shows how $\mathbb{C}_A$ is generated given a workflow W, availability configuration θ, resiliency function δ, size bound q, and resiliency threshold r. The set $\mathbb{C}_A$ contains subsets of $V \setminus A$ where V is the set of all possible authorisation constraints and A is the set of current authorisation constraints. Two algorithms similar in nature to Algorithm 1 exist for computing $\mathbb{C}_S$, and $\mathbb{C}_B$ which contain subsets of S and B respectively.

WRAD Analysis Process. Figure 1 shows the main components of WRAD and the resiliency analysis process: (1) a textual description of a workflow W and availability configuration θ (e.g., Fig. 2) is inputted to WRAD together with a size bound q and resiliency threshold r; (2) the workflow encoder automatically encodes the workflow description as a Markov decision process (MDP) written in the state-based PRISM language; (3) the probabilistic model checker PRISM

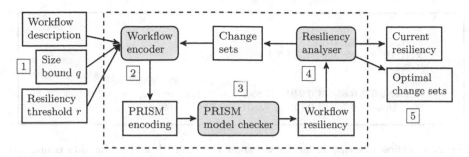

Fig. 1. Analysis process of WRAD which takes a workflow description, size bound q, and resiliency threshold r as input and outputs current resiliency and optimal change sets for security constraints.

solves the MDP encoding to compute the current resiliency of the workflow; (4) the resiliency analyser generates the optimal change sets for security constraints A, S and B; (5) the resiliency analyser outputs both the current resiliency of the workflow and the optimal change sets. We now describe the main components of WRAD in more detail.

Workflow Description. WRAD requires as input a textual *workflow descrip-tion* expressing a workflow $W = ((T, \prec), U, (A, S, B))$ and availability configuration θ. A workflow description is written as a six line (.wrad) file, which can be mapped directly from the formal definitions of W and θ given in Sect. 2:

$\quad W_i \;\rightarrow\; \text{w}i$ is a workflow identifier.

$\quad (T, \prec) \;\rightarrow\; n : |i, j| \ldots |i', j'|$ where $n = |T|$ is the number of tasks and for each pair $|i, j|$, $t_i \prec t_j$.

$\quad A \;\rightarrow\; k : |i, j| \ldots |i', j'|$ where $k = |U|$ is the number of users and for each pair $|i, j|$, $(t_i, u_j) \in A$.

$\quad S \;\rightarrow\; |i, j| \ldots |i', j'|$ where for each pair $|i, j|$, $(t_i, u_j) \in S$.

$\quad B \;\rightarrow\; |i, j| \ldots |i', j'|$ where for each pair $|i, j|$, $(t_i, u_j) \in B$.

$\quad \theta \;\rightarrow\; |i, j, m| \ldots |i', j', m'|$ where for each triple $|i, j, m|$, $\theta(i, u_j) = m$.

Figure 2 provides a workflow description for a small workflow example W_1 and availability configuration θ_1 we use throughout the remainder of this section to illustrate various concepts. The workflow description file is inputted to WRAD at the command line together with a size bound q and resiliency threshold r.

Workflow Encoder. In [6] we showed that computing the optimal policy of a Markov decision process (MDP) modelling a workflow's assignment process is

```
w1
5 : |1, 2|1, 4|2, 3|3, 5|4, 5|
3 : |1, 1|1, 2|1, 3|2, 3|3, 1|3, 2|3, 3|4, 1|4, 2|5, 1|5, 2|
|1, 2|2, 3|2, 4|3, 5|
|3, 4|
|0, 1, 0.96|0, 2, 0.86|0, 3, 0.94|1, 1, 0.89|1, 2, 0.85|1, 3, 0.91|2, 1, 0.80|2, 2, 0.85|2, 3, 0.89
|3, 1, 0.69|3, 2, 0.74|3, 3, 0.75|4, 1, 0.64|4, 2, 0.72|4, 3, 0.69|
```

Fig. 2. Workflow description file for workflow example W_1 and availability configuration θ_1, which is inputted to WRAD for resiliency evaluation.

equivalent to finding a plan maximising the MDP's value function. The value function returns $0 \leq v \leq 1$ where v indicates the resiliency of the workflow and provides an implementation of the resiliency function δ. WRAD encodes the inputted workflow description as an MDP in the state-based PRISM language, an example of which can be found in [7]. Each state of the MDP encoded in PRISM is essentially a tuple of the form (a, t, P, θ) where: (1) a is the current action being performed (e.g., select task t, find valid users for t, assign t); (2) t is the 'ready' task selected for assignment; (3) P is a partial plan indicating all valid task assignments previous to t; (4) θ is the users' availability configuration. A set of modules in the PRISM encoding contain commands which update a, t or P when guards placed on those commands become true. The commands essentially transition the encoded MDP to a next valid state. The availability configuration θ is encoded as a set of modules, one per user, which update each user's probabilistic availability after each task assignment accordingly.

PRISM Model Checker. There are many ways to solve an MDP including dynamic programming (e.g. value iteration) [4]. This technique is provided by the probabilistic model checking tool PRISM enables the specification, construction and analysis of probabilistic models such as MDPs [5]. PRISM is an intuitive choice as it can model both non-deterministic (e.g., task selection) and probabilistic (e.g. user availability) choice, and gives an efficient way to solve an MDP. WRAD inputs an MDP encoding into PRISM which verifies the maximum probability that a state can eventually be reached such that a valid and complete plan exists, that is all tasks are assigned a user and all constraints are satisfied. This property is inputted into PRISM as `Pmax=? [F "plan"]`, where F is the eventually operator.

Policy Analyser. The policy analyser outputs the current resiliency of a workflow W and the sets $\mathbb{C}_A$, $\mathbb{C}_S$, and $\mathbb{C}_B$ of all optimal change sets for the three types of security constraint we consider. Figure 3 illustrates Algorithm 1 for our example workflow W_1 where the size bound $q = 3$, resiliency threshold $r = 0.55$, and resiliency $\delta(W_1, \theta) = 0.4325$. WRAD generates three optimal authorisation constraint change sets where $\mathbb{C}_A =$

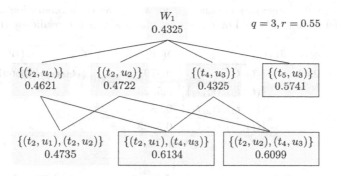

$$W_1$$
$$0.4325 \qquad q = 3, r = 0.55$$

| $\{(t_2, u_1)\}$ | $\{(t_2, u_2)\}$ | $\{(t_4, u_3)\}$ | $\{(t_5, u_3)\}$ |
| 0.4621 | 0.4722 | 0.4325 | 0.5741 |

| $\{(t_2, u_1), (t_2, u_2)\}$ | $\{(t_2, u_1), (t_4, u_3)\}$ | $\{(t_2, u_2), (t_4, u_3)\}$ |
| 0.4735 | 0.6134 | 0.6099 |

Fig. 3. Illustration of algorithm to find optimal change sets C_A of size $q \leq 3$ where resiliency $\delta(W_1 + C_A, \theta) \geq 0.55$.

$\{\{(t_5, u_3)\}, \{(t_2, u_1), (t_4, u_3)\}, \{(t_2, u_2), (t_4, u_3)\}\}$. Note Algorithm 1 need only consider change sets of sizes 1 and 2. Table 1 shows all optimal change sets C_S and C_B for W_1 also generated by WRAD. We assume the final selection of which change set to implement will be the choice of the security policy designer. For instance the designer may select $\{(t_5, u_3)\}$ from $\mathbb{C}_A$ to minimise changes to the security policy, or $\{(t_2, u_1), (t_4, u_3)\}$ to maximise resiliency, or $\{(t_2, u_2), (t_4, u_3)\}$ because users u_2 and u_3 are only qualified to perform t_2 and t_4 respectively.

Computation Time. Computation time for the above analysis was 39.4 s running WRAD on a MacBook Pro with 2.7 GHz Intel Core i5 processor and 16 MB RAM, running OS X version 10.11.4. and PRISM version 4.3.1. To give an indication of how computation time can change we analysed workflow $W_2 = W_1 + \{(t_2, u_2), (t_4, u_3)\}$ with $r = 0.70$. A single change set of binding constraints $\{(t_3, t_4)\}$ was found in a total computation time of 10.4 s. Next analysing $W_3 = W_2 - \{(t_3, t_4)\}$ with $r = 0.80$ found four singleton change sets for authorisation constraints in 21.8 s. In [7] we observed resiliency computation time is closely coupled with the complexity of a workflow in terms of its number of tasks, users and constraints. We showed that adding or removing particular sets of constraints can increase resiliency computation time whilst other sets may reduce it.

4   Final Remarks

Related and Future Work. To the best of our knowledge no tool support exists for policy designers to automatically evaluate workflow resiliency and compute optimal security constraint changes. Existing work on workflow resiliency has focused on understanding its complexity [11] and finding efficient solutions to the problem [1]. The scalability of WRAD is bounded by the size of models PRISM can evaluate, that is the number of reachable states in the MDP encoding. Although no definitive answer is provided, the developers of PRISM suggest

Table 1. Optimal change sets C_S and C_B for workflow W_1's separation and binding constraints, where q is a bound on change set size and r is the resiliency threshold.

	q	r	$\delta(W_1, \theta)$	C_S	$\delta(W_1 - C_S, \theta)$	C_B	$\delta(W_1 - C_B, \theta)$
W_1	3	0.55	0.4325	$\{(t_3, t_5)\}$	0.5792	$\{(t_3, t_4)\}$	0.5697
				$\{(t_1, t_2), (t_2, t_3)\}$	0.5823		
				$\{(t_1, t_2), (t_2, t_4)\}$	0.5823		
				$\{(t_2, t_3), (t_2, t_4)\}$	0.5823		

models with up to 10^8 states can be evaluated on a 'typical PC'. Encoding the example workflow from Sect. 3 into PRISM produces a model with 760 states. We look to carry out scalability testing of WRAD to understand the limitations on resiliency evaluation in terms of a workflow's complexity, and explore ways our encoding in PRISM can be refined to reduce the reachable state space. Scalability testing will be informed by understanding more the size and complexity of workflows being designed in real-life scenarios. Any scalability restrictions may be overcome by implementing an approach inspired by the work in [2] which connects security policies across modular workflows. We also look to implement finding optimal change sets of mixed constraint types and handling workflows with choice as defined in [9].

Conclusion. Workflow resiliency provides a measure of workflow productivity when assuming users may become unavailable at runtime. In this paper we have introduced a new tool *Workflow Resiliency Analysis and Design* (WRAD) for workflow designers to automatically evaluate the resiliency of security constrained workflows and help reach acceptable productivity-security trade-offs before execution. WRAD computes optimal changes to three types of security constraints which assure a required resiliency threshold is reached.

References

1. Crampton, J., Gutin, G., Watrigant, R.: An approach to parameterized resiliency problems using integer linear programming. CoRR, abs/1605.08738 (2016)
2. dos Santos, D.R., Ponta, S.E., Ranise, S.: Modular synthesis of enforcement mechanisms for the workflow satisfiability problem: scalability and reusability. In: SACMAT 2016 (2016, to appear)
3. Georgakopoulos, D., Hornick, M., Sheth, A.: An overview of workflow management: from process modeling to workflow automation infrastructure. Distrib. Parallel Databases **3**(2), 119–153 (1995)
4. Howard, R.A.: Dynamic Programming and Markov Processes. MIT Press, Cambridge (1960)
5. Kwiatkowska, M., Norman, G., Parker, D.: PRISM 4.0: verification of probabilistic real-time systems. In: Gopalakrishnan, G., Qadeer, S. (eds.) CAV 2011. LNCS, vol. 6806, pp. 585–591. Springer, Heidelberg (2011)

6. Mace, J.C., Morisset, C., van Moorsel, A.P.A.: Quantitative workflow resiliency. In: Kutyłowski, M., Vaidya, J. (eds.) ICAIS 2014, Part I. LNCS, vol. 8712, pp. 344–361. Springer, Heidelberg (2014)
7. Mace, J.C., Morisset, C., van Moorsel, A.P.A.: Impact of policy design on workflow resiliency computation time. In: Campos, J., Haverkort, B.R. (eds.) QEST 2015. LNCS, vol. 9259, pp. 244–259. Springer, Heidelberg (2015)
8. Mace, J.C., Morisset, C., van Moorsel, A.P.A.: Modelling user availability in workflow resiliency analysis. In: HotSoS 2015, pp. 1–10 (2015)
9. Mace, J.C., Morisset, C., van Moorsel, A.P.A.: Resiliency variance in workflows with choice. In: Fantechi, A., Pelliccione, P. (eds.) SERENE 2015. LNCS, vol. 9274, pp. 128–143. Springer, Heidelberg (2015)
10. Post, G.V., Kagan, A.: Evaluating information security tradeoffs: restricting access can interfere with user tasks. Comput. Secur. **26**(3), 229–237 (2007)
11. Wang, Q., Li, N.: Satisfiability, resiliency in workflow authorization systems. ACM Trans. Inf. Syst. Secur. **13**(4), 40:1–40:35 (2010)

Designing a Resilient Deployment and Reconfiguration Infrastructure for Remotely Managed Cyber-Physical Systems

Subhav Pradhan[✉], Abhishek Dubey, and Aniruddha Gokhale

Department of Electrical Engineering and Computer Science,
Vanderbilt University, Nashville, TN, USA
{subhav.m.pradhan,abhishek.dubey,a.gokhale}@vanderbilt.edu

Abstract. Multi-module Cyber-Physical Systems (CPS), such as satellite clusters, swarms of Unmanned Aerial Vehicles (UAV), and fleets of Unmanned Underwater Vehicles (UUV) provide a CPS cluster-as-a-service for CPS applications. The distributed and remote nature of these systems often necessitates the use of Deployment and Configuration (D&C) services to manage the lifecycle of these applications. Fluctuating resources, volatile cluster membership and changing environmental conditions necessitate resilience. Thus, the D&C infrastructure does not only have to undertake basic management actions, such as activation of new applications and deactivation of existing applications, but also has to autonomously reconfigure existing applications to mitigate failures including D&C infrastructure failures. This paper describes the design and architectural considerations to realize such a D&C infrastructure for component-based distributed systems. Experimental results demonstrating the autonomous resilience capabilities are presented.

Keywords: Self-reconfiguration · Autonomous resilience · Deployment and reconfiguration · Component-based distributed systems

1 Introduction

Cyber-Physical Systems (CPS) are a class of distributed, real-time and embedded systems that tightly integrate the cyber dimension with the physical dimension whereby the physical system and its constraints control the way the cyber infrastructure operates and in turn the latter controls the physical objects [10]. Fractionated spacecraft, swarms of Unmanned Aerial Vehicles (UAVs), and fleets of Unmanned Underwater Vehicles (UUVs), represent a new class of highly dynamic, cluster-based, distributed CPS. These systems often operate in unwieldy environments where resources are very limited, the dynamic nature of the system results in ever-changing cluster properties, such as membership, failures and fluctuation in resource availability is common, and human intervention to address these problems is rarely feasible.

© Springer International Publishing Switzerland 2016
I. Crnkovic and E. Troubitsyna (Eds.): SERENE 2016, LNCS 9823, pp. 88–104, 2016.
DOI: 10.1007/978-3-319-45892-2_7

Resilience is thus a key requirement for such cyber physical systems. A resilient system is defined as a system that is capable of maintaining and recovering its functionality when faced with failures and anomalies. Since human intervention is extremely limited resilience should be autonomous. As such, resilience can be provided either by using redundancy or by using a self-reconfiguration (self-adaptation) mechanism. In this paper, we are concerned with the self-reconfiguration aspect. The goal is to achieve a self-adaptive system [20] for which following requirements must be met:

– Requirement 1: an adaptation capability that can maintain and recover the system's functionality by adapting applications hosted on the system.
– Requirement 2: the adaptation capability itself should be resilient such that any failure or anomaly does not effect the adaptability of the overall system.

We are concerned with those CPS where the cyber functionalities are implemented using the Component-Based Software Engineering (CBSE) [8] approach, where applications are realized by composing, deploying and configuring software components with well-defined interaction ports. A number of different component models (providing the interaction and execution semantics for the components) exist: Fractal [3], CORBA Component Model (CCM) [14], LwCCM [13] etc. Similarly, there exists different Deployment and Configuration (D&C) infrastructures that are compatible with different component modes.

Since the D&C capability is a key artifact of any component-based system, we surmise that resilience can be improved by enhancing the D&C infrastructure so that it can provide the adaptation capability. This means the D&C infrastructure should not only be able to manage the lifecycle of applications, it should also be able to reconfigure existing applications and do so in a resilient manner [19]. However, existing D&C infrastructures do not support both these requirements. Either they are not capable of performing runtime reconfiguration [5,7,16,17] or others that are capable of performing runtime reconfiguration are themselves not resilient [1,2].

This paper overcomes limitations of existing solutions by presenting a novel and resilient D&C infrastructure that satisfies both the aforementioned requirements. In doing so, we make the following contributions:

– We present the key challenges in achieving a resilient D&C infrastructure.
– We present an architecture for a resilient D&C infrastructure that addresses these key challenges.
– We present experimental results to demonstrate application adaptability of our new D&C infrastructure.

The remainder of this paper is organized as follows: Sect. 2 presents existing work related to this paper and explains how our approach is different; Sect. 3 describes the target system model, D&C model, and fault model to present the problem at hand; Sect. 4 presents the key challenges that needs to be addressed in order to achieve a resilient D&C infrastructure; Sect. 5 presents detailed description of our solution and how it addresses aforementioned challenges; Sect. 6

presents experimental results; finally, Sect. 7 provides concluding remarks and alludes to future work.

2   Related Work

Deployment and configuration of component-based software is a well-researched field with existing works primarily focusing on D&C infrastructure for grid computing and Distributed Real-time Embedded (DRE) systems. Both Deploy-Ware [7] and GoDIET [5] are general-purpose deployment frameworks targeted towards deploying large-scale, hierarchically composed, Fractal [3] component model-based applications in a grid environment. However, both of these deployment frameworks are not resilient and they lack support for application reconfiguration. As such, they do not satisfy the two requirements essential for realizing autonomous resilience.

The Object Management Group (OMG) has standardized the Deployment and Configuration (D&C) specification [15]. Our prior work on the Deployment And Configuration Engine (DAnCE) [17] describes a concrete realization of the OMG D&C specification for the Lightweight CORBA Component Model (LwCCM) [13]. LE-DAnCE [17] and F6 DeploymentManager [6] are some of our other previous works that extend the OMG's D&C specification. LE-DAnCE deploys and configures components based on the Lightweight CORBA Component Model [13] whereas the F6 Deployment Manager does the same for components based on F6-COM component model [16]. The F6 Deployment Manager, in particular, focused on the deployment of real-time component-based applications in highly dynamic DRE systems, such as fractionated spacecraft. However, similar to the work mentioned above, these infrastructures also lack support for application adaptation and D&C infrastructure resilience.

A significant amount of research exists in the field of dynamic reconfiguration of component-based applications. In [2], the authors present a tool called Planit for deployment and reconfiguration of component-based applications. Planit uses AI-based planner to come up with application deployment plan for both - initial deployment, and subsequent dynamic reconfigurations. Planit is based on a *sense-plan-act* model for fault detection, diagnosis and reconfiguration to recover from failures. Another work presented in [1], supports dynamic reconfiguration of applications based on J2EE components. Although these solutions support application reconfiguration, none of them focus on resilience of their respective adaptation engine.

The authors in [4] present the DEECo (Distributed Emergent Ensembles of Components) component model, which is based on the concept of Ensemble-Based Component System (EBCS). In general, this approach replaces traditional explicit component architecture by the composition of components into *ensembles*. An ensemble is an implicit, inherently dynamic group of components where each component is an autonomic entity facilitating self-adaptive and resilient operation. In [9], authors present a formal foundation for ensemble modeling. However, they do not focus on the management infrastructure required to deploy and reconfigure these components.

3   Problem Description

This section describes the problem at hand by first presenting the target system model. Second, we present the Deployment and Configuration (D&C) model. Third, we present the fault model related to system model. Finally, we describe the problem of self-adaptation in the context of the D&C infrastructure.

3.1   System Model

The work described in this paper assumes a distributed CPS consisting of multiple interconnected computing nodes that host distributed applications. For example, we consider a distributed system of fractionated spacecraft [6] that hosts mission-critical component-based applications with mixed criticality levels and security requirements. Fractionated spacecraft represents a highly dynamic CPS because it is a distributed system composed of nodes (individual satellites) that can join and leave a cluster at any time resulting in *volatile group membership* characteristics.

A distributed application in our system model is a graph of software components that are partitioned into processes[1] and hosted within a "component" server. This graph is then mapped to interconnected computing nodes. The interaction relationship between the components are defined using established interaction patterns such as (a) synchronous and asynchronous remote method invocation, and (b) group-based publish-subscribe communication.

3.2   Deployment and Configuration Model

To deploy distributed component-based applications[2] onto a target environment, the system needs to provide a software deployment service. A Deployment and Configuration (D&C) infrastructure serves this purpose; it is responsible for instantiating application components on individual nodes, configuring their interactions, and then managing their lifecycle. The D&C infrastructure should be viewed as a distributed infrastructure composed of multiple deployment entities, with one entity residing on each node.

OMG's D&C specification [15] is a standard for deployment and configuration of component-based applications. Our prior work on the Locality-Enabled Deployment And Configuration Engine (LE-DAnCE) [17] is an open-source implementation of this specification. As shown in Fig. 1, LE-DAnCE implements a strict two-layered approach comprising different kinds of Deployment Managers (DM). A DM is a deployment entity. The Cluster Deployment Manager (CDM) is the single orchestrator that controls cluster-wide deployment process by coordinating deployment among different Node Deployment Managers (NDM).

---

[1] Components hosted within a process are located within the same address space.
[2] Although we use the component model described in [13], our work is not constrained by this choice and can be applied to other component models as well.

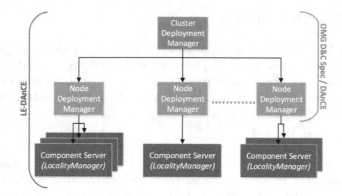

Fig. 1. Orchestrated deployment approach in LE-DAnCE [17]

Similarly, a NDM controls node-specific deployment process by instantiating component servers that create and manage application components.

LE-DAnCE, however, is not resilient and it does not support run-time application adaptation as well. Therefore, our work presented in this paper modifies and extends LE-DAnCE to achieve a D&C infrastructure capable of facilitating autonomous resilience.

3.3 Fault Model

Failure can be defined as a loss of functionality in a system. The goal of a resilient system is to ensure that subsystem or component-level faults do not lead to loss of system functionality, i.e. a failure, for an unacceptable length of time. The system is expected to recover from a failure, and the threshold on time to recovery is typically a requirement on the system. Recovering from failures involves adapting the failed subsystem such that its functionality is restored. For example, in software intensive systems this process primarily involves adaptation of applications that are deployed in the failed subsystem.

In the systems under consideration, we observe that subsystem failures can be categorized as infrastructure or application failures. Infrastructure failures are failures that arise due to faults affecting a system's network, participating nodes, or processes that are running in these nodes. Usually, infrastructure failures can be classified as *primary failures*. Whereas, application failures are failures pertaining to the application itself. We assume that application components have been thoroughly tested before deployment and therefore classify application failures as *secondary failures* caused due to infrastructure failures.

3.4 Problem Statement

For the prescribed system and fault model, the D&C infrastructure should, first and foremost, be capable of dealing with infrastructure failures. Conceptually, a

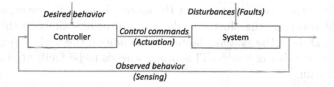

Fig. 2. Self-adaptive system as a control system

resilient infrastructure can be modeled as a resilient feedback control loop that observes the system state and compensates for disturbances in the system to achieve a desired behavior as shown in Fig. 2.

To find similarities with the traditional self-adaptive loop and the system under discussion, consider that a failure in the infrastructure can be considered as a disturbance. This failure can be detected by behavior such as "node is responding to pings" (indicating there is infrastructure failure) or not. Once the failure has been detected, the loss of functionality needs to be restored by facilitating reconfiguration, for example, re-allocating components to a functioning node, etc.; this needs to be done in a resilient manner. The presence of the controller and its actuation ability enables the self-adaptive property needed of an autonomously resilient system.

4   Key Considerations and Challenges

To correctly provide resilient D&C services to a CPS cluster, the D&C infrastructure must resolve the challenges described below:

Challenge 1 (Distributed group membership): Recall that the CPS domain illustrates a highly dynamic environment in terms of resources that are available for application deployment: nodes may leave unexpectedly as a result of a failure or as part of a planned or unplanned partitioning of the cluster, and nodes may also join the cluster as they recover from faults or are brought online. To provide resilient behavior, the DMs in the cluster must be aware of changes in group membership, i.e., they must be able to detect when one of their peers has left the group (either as a result of a fault or planned partitioning) and when new peers join the cluster.

Challenge 2 (Leader election): As faults occur in CPS, a resilient system must make definitive decisions about the nature of that fault and the best course of action necessary to mitigate and recover from that fault. Since CPS clusters often operate in mission- or safety-critical environments where delayed reaction to faults can severely compromise the safety of the cluster, such decisions must be made in a timely manner. In order to accommodate this requirement, the system should always have a *cluster leader* that will be responsible for making decisions and performing other tasks that impact the entire cluster.[3] However, a node that hosts the DM acting as the cluster leader can fail at any time; in this scenario, the remaining DMs in the system should decide among themselves regarding the identity of the new cluster leader. This process needs to be facilitated by a leader election algorithm.

Challenge 3 (Deployment sequencing): Applications in CPS may be composed of several cooperating components with complex internal dependencies that are distributed across several nodes. Deployment of such an application requires that deployment activities across several nodes proceed in a synchronized manner. For example, connections between two dependent components cannot be established until both components have been successfully instantiated. Depending on the application, some might require stronger sequencing semantics whereby all components of the application need to be activated simultaneously.

Challenge 4 (D&C State Preservation): Nodes in a CPS may fail at any time and for any reason; a D&C infrastructure capable of supporting such a cluster must be able to reconstitute those portions of the distributed application that were deployed on the failed node. Supporting resilience requires the D&C infrastructure to keep track of the global system state, which consists of (a) component-to-application mapping, (b) component-to-implementation mapping[4], (c) component-to-node mapping, (d) inter-component connection information, (e) component state information, and (f) the current group membership information. Such state preservation is particularly important for a new leader.

5   A Resilient D&C Infrastructure

Figure 3 presents an overview of our solution. Infrastructure failures are detected using the Group Membership Monitor (GMM). Application failure detection is outside the scope of this paper, however, we refer readers to our earlier work [11] in this area. The controller is in fact a collection of DMs working together to deploy and configure as well as reconfigure application components. The specific actuation commands are redeployment actions taken by the DMs.

5.1   Solution Architecture

Figure 4 presents the architecture of our resilient D&C infrastructure. Each node consists of a single Deployment Manager (DM). A collection of these DMs forms the overall D&C infrastructure. Our approach supports distributed, peer-to-peer application deployment, where each node controls its local deployment process. Each DM spawns one or more Component Servers (CSs), which are processes responsible for managing the lifecycle of application components. Note that our

---

[3] Achieving a consensus-based agreement for each adaptation decision would likely be inefficient and violate the real-time constraints of the cluster.

[4] A component can have multiple implementations.

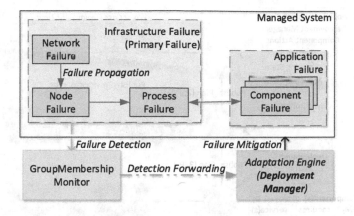

Fig. 3. Overview of a resilient D&C infrastructure.

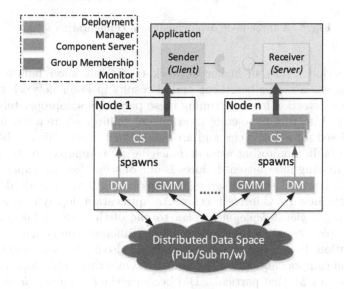

Fig. 4. Architecture of a resilience D&C infrastructure.

approach does not follow a centralized coordinator for deployment actions; rather the DMs are independent and use a publish/subscribe middleware to communicate with each other.

In our architecture, we use the GMM to maintain up-to-date group membership information, and to detect failures via a periodic heartbeat monitoring mechanism. The failure detection aspect of GMM relies on two important parameters – *heartbeat period* and *failure monitoring period*. These configurable parameters allows us to control how often each DM asserts its liveliness and how often each DM monitors failure. For a given failure monitoring period, a lower

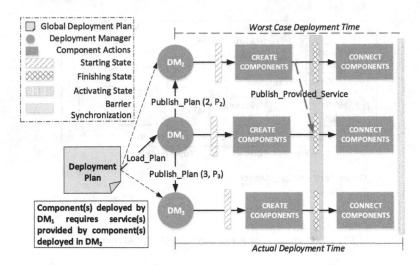

Fig. 5. A three-node deployment and configuration setup

heartbeat period results in higher network traffic but lower failure detection latency, whereas a higher heartbeat period results in lower network traffic but higher failure detection latency. Tuning these parameters appropriately can also enable the architecture to tolerate intermittent failures where a few heartbeats are only missed for a few cycles and are established later. This can be done by making the fault monitoring window much larger compared to the heartbeat period. Addressing intermittent failures is out of scope for this paper.

Figure 5 shows an event diagram demonstrating a three node deployment process of our new D&C infrastructure. An application deployment is initiated by submitting a *global deployment plan* to one of the three DMs. This global deployment plan contains information about different components (and their implementation) that make up an application. It also contains information about how different components should be connected. Once this global deployment plan is received by a DM, that particular DM becomes the *deployment leader* for that particular deployment plan. A deployment leader is only responsible for initiating the deployment process for a given deployment plan by analyzing the plan and allocating deployment actions to other DMs in the system. The deployment leader is not responsible for other cluster-wide operations such as *failure mitigation*; these cluster-wide operations are handled by a *cluster leader*. Two different global deployment plans can be deployed by two different deployment leaders since we do not require a centralized coordinator in our approach.

Deployment and configuration in our scheme is a multi-staged approach. Table 1 lists the different D&C stages in our approach. The INITIAL stage is where a deployment plan gets submitted to a DM and ACTIVATED stage is where the application components in the deployment plan is active. In the rest of this section, we describe how information in this table is used in our solution to address the key challenges.

Table 1. D&C Stages

Stage	Description
INITIAL	(1) Global deployment plan is provided to one of the DMs
	(2) DM that is provided with a global deployment plan becomes the leader DM and loads that deployment plan and stores it in a binary format
PREPARING	(1) Plan loaded in the previous stage is split into node-specific plans and they are published to the distributed data space using pub/sub middleware
	(2) Node-specific plans published above are received by all DMs and only the ones that are relevant are further split into component server (CS)-specific plans
STARTING	(1) CS-specific plans created in the previous stage are used to create CSs (if required) and components
	(2) For components that provide service via a *facet*, the DM will publish its connection information so that other components that require this service can connect to it using their *receptacle*. This connection however is not established in this stage
	(3) In this stage, barrier synchronization is performed to make sure that no individual DMs can advance to the next stage before all of the DMs have reached this point
FINISHING	(1) Components created in the previous stage are connected (if required). In order for this to happen, the components that require a service use connection information provided in the previous stage to make facet-receptacle connections
ACTIVATING	(1) Synchronization stage to make sure all components are created and connected (if required) before activation
ACTIVATED	(1) Stage where a deployment plan is activated by activating all the related components
	(2) At this point all application components are running
TEARDOWN	(1) De-activation stage

5.2 Addressing Resilient D&C Challenges

Resolving Challenge 1 (Distributed Group Membership): To support distributed group membership, our solution requires a mechanism that allows detection of joining members and leaving members. To that end our solution uses a *discovery mechanism* to detect the former and a *failure detection mechanism* to detect the latter as described below.

Discovery Mechanism: Since our solution approach relies on an underlying pub/sub middleware, the discovery of nodes joining the cluster leverages existing discovery services provided by the pub/sub middleware. To that end we have used OpenDDS (http://www.opendds.org) – an open source pub/sub middleware that implements OMG's Data Distribution Service (DDS) specification [12]. To be more specific, we use the Real-Time Publish Subscribe (RTPS) peer-to-peer discovery mechanism specified by DDS.

Failure Detection Mechanism: To detect the loss of existing members, we need a failure detection mechanism that detects different kinds of failures. In our architecture this functionality is provided by the GMM. The GMM residing on each node uses a simple heartbeat-based protocol to detect DM (process) failure. Recall that any node failure, including the ones caused due to network failure, results in the failure of its DM. This means that our failure detection service uses the same mechanism to detect all three different kinds of infrastructure failures.

Resolving Challenge 2 (Leader Election): Leader election is required in order to tolerate cluster leader failure. We do this by implementing a rank-based leader election algorithm. Each DM is assigned a unique numeric rank value and this information is published by each DM as part of its heartbeat. Initially the DM with the least rank will be picked as the cluster leader. If the cluster leader fails, each of the other DMs in the cluster will check their group membership table and determine if it is the new leader. Since, we associate a unique rank with each DM, only one DM will be elected as the new leader.

Resolving Challenge 3 (Proper Sequencing of Deployment): Our D&C infrastructure implements deployment synchronization using a distributed *barrier synchronization* algorithm. This mechanism is specifically used during the STARTING stage of the D&C process to make sure that all DMs are in the STARTING stage before any of them can advance to the FINISHING stage. This synchronization is performed to ensure that all connection information of all the components that provide a service is published to the distributed data space before components that require a service try to establish a connection. We realize that this might be too strong of a requirement and therefore we intend to further relax this requirement by making sure that only components that require a service wait for synchronization. In addition, our current solution also uses barrier synchronization in the ACTIVATING stage to make sure all DMs advance to the ACTIVATED stage simultaneously. This particular synchronization ensures the simultaneous activation of a distributed application.

Resolving Challenge 4 (D&C State Preservation): In our current implementation, once a deployment plan is split into node-specific deployment plans, all of the DMs receive the node-specific deployment plans. Although any further action on a node-specific deployment plan is only taken by a DM if that plan belongs to the node in which the DM is deployed, all DMs store each and every node-specific deployment plans in its memory. This ensures that deployment-related information is replicated throughout a cluster thereby preventing single point of failure. However, this approach is vulnerable to DM process failures since deployment information is stored in memory. To resolve this issue, we are currently working on extending our solution to use a persistent backend distributed database to store deployment information.

6   Experimental Results

This section presents results to demonstrate the autonomous resilience capabilities of our D&C infrastructure. We show how our resilient D&C infrastructure adapts applications as well as itself after encountering a node failure during deployment-time, and runtime.

6.1   Testbed

For all of our experiments, we used a multi-computing node cluster setup that consisted of three nodes, each with a 1.6 GHz Atom N270 processor and 1 GB of RAM. Each node runs vanilla Ubuntu server image 13.04 which uses Linux kernel version 3.8.0-19.

The application we used for self-adaptability experiments presented in Sects. 6.2 and 6.3 is a simple two-component client-server experiment presented earlier in Fig. 4. The Sender component (client) is initially deployed in node-1, the Receiver component (server) is initially deployed in node-2, and node-3 has nothing deployed on it. For both experiments, we consider node-2 to be the node that fails. Furthermore, we configure our infrastructure with heartbeat period set to 2 s and failure monitoring period set to 5 s.

6.2   Node Failure During Deployment-Time

Figure 6 presents a time sequence graph of how our D&C infrastructure adapts itself to tolerate failures during deployment-time. As can be seen, node 2 and therefore DM-2 fails at Event 5. Once the failure is detected by both DM-1 in node-1 and DM-3 in node-3, DM-1 being the leader initiates the recovery process (Event 6 - Event 7). During this time, DM-1 determines the part of the application that was supposed to be deployed by DM-2 in node-2, which is the Receiver component. Once DM-1 determines this information, it completes the recovery process by republishing information about the failure affected part of application (Receiver component) to DM-3. Finally, DM-3 deploys the Receiver component in node-3 and after this point, the deployment process resumes normally.

6.3   Node Failure During Application Run-Time

Figure 7 presents a time sequence graph that demonstrates how our D&C infrastructure adapts applications at run-time to tolerate run-time node failures. Unlike the scenario presented before where the initial deployment of the application has to be adapted to tolerate deployment-time failure, here the initial deployment completes successfully at Event 19 after which the application is

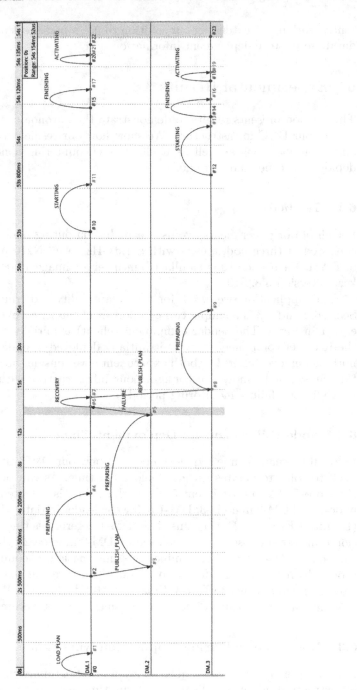

Fig. 6. Node failure during application deployment time.

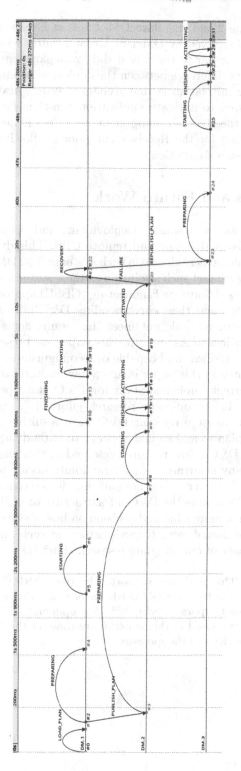

Fig. 7. Node failure during application run-time

active. However, node-2 and therefore DM-2 fails at Event 20 and the notification of this failure is received by DM-1 at Event 21 after which DM-1 performs the recovery process similar to the way it did for deployment-time failure.

The one significant difference between the deployment-time failure mitigation and run-time failure mitigation is that dynamic reconfiguration of application components is required to mitigate application run-time failure. To elaborate, once DM-3 deploys the Receiver component in node-3 it needs to publish new connection information for the Receiver component allowing DM-1 to update Sender the component's connection.

7   Conclusions and Future Work

This paper described a resilient Deployment and Configuration (D&C) infrastructure for highly dynamic and remote CPS. This dynamic and remote nature calls for autonomous resilience in such systems. The D&C infrastructure is the right artifact to architect such a solution as these systems are commonly built using Component-Based Software Engineering (CBSE) approach using appropriate component models and their corresponding D&C infrastructure. However, existing D&C infrastructures do not meet the requirements essential to facilitate autonomous resilience. As such, in this paper we presented a novel D&C infrastructure that is resilient and capable of reconfiguring existing applications.

The work presented in this paper incurs a few limitations: (1) As mentioned in Sect. 5.2, our current implementation for D&C state preservation is sufficient but not ideal. In our on-going research effort [18], we look into using a distributed database to store relevant D&C state resulting in a stateless D&C infrastructure. We plan to add similar concept to extend the work presented in this paper. (2) The D&C infrastructure presented in this paper performs reconfiguration without any smartness, i.e., we randomly decide where a component should be migrated. However, this is not sufficient for systems that can host multiple applications. We require the D&C infrastructure to utilize available system information to make a more educated decision on how a system should be reconfigured. Again, some initial work towards achieving such an infrastructure has been presented as part of our on-going research effort [18].

Acknowledgment. This work was supported by the DARPA System F6 Program under contract NNA11AC08C, USAF/AFRL under Cooperative Agreement FA8750-13-2-0050, and Siemens Corporate Technology. Any opinions, findings, and conclusions or recommendations expressed in this material are those of the author(s) and do not necessarily reflect the views of the sponsors.

References

1. Akkerman, A., Totok, A.A., Karamcheti, V.: Infrastructure for automatic dynamic deployment of J2EE applications in distributed environments. In: Dearle, A., Savani, R. (eds.) CD 2005. LNCS, vol. 3798, pp. 17–32. Springer, Heidelberg (2005)
2. Arshad, N., Heimbigner, D., Wolf, A.L.: Deployment and dynamic reconfiguration planning for distributed software systems. In: Proceedings of 15th IEEE International Conference on Tools with Artificial Intelligence, pp. 39–46. IEEE (2003)
3. Bruneton, E., Coupaye, T., Leclercq, M., Quéma, V., Stefani, J.B.: The fractal component model and its support in java. Softw. Pract. Exp. **36**(11–12), 1257–1284 (2006)
4. Bures, T., Gerostathopoulos, I., Hnetynka, P., Keznikl, J., Kit, M., Plasil, F.: Deeco: an ensemble-based component system. In: Proceedings of the 16th International ACM Sigsoft Symposium on Component-Based Software Engineering, pp. 81–90. ACM (2013)
5. Caron, E., Chouhan, P.K., Dail, H.: Godiet: a deployment tool for distributed middleware on grid'5000. Ph.D. thesis, INRIA (2006)
6. Dubey, A., Emfinger, W., Gokhale, A., Karsai, G., Otte, W., Parsons, J., Szabo, C., Coglio, A., Smith, E., Bose, P.: A software platform for fractionated spacecraft. In: Proceedings of the IEEE Aerospace Conference 2012, pp. 1–20. IEEE, Big Sky, MT, USA, March 2012
7. Flissi, A., Dubus, J., Dolet, N., Merle, P.: Deploying on the grid with deployware. In: 8th IEEE International Symposium on Cluster Computing and the Grid, CCGRID 2008, pp. 177–184. IEEE (2008)
8. Heineman, G.T., Councill, W.T. (eds.): Component-based Software Engineering: Putting the Pieces Together. Addison-Wesley Longman Publishing Co., Inc., Boston (2001)
9. Hennicker, Rolf, Klarl, Annabelle: Foundations for ensemble modeling – the HELENA approach. In: Iida, Shusaku, Meseguer, José, Ogata, Kazuhiro (eds.) Specification, Algebra, and Software. LNCS, vol. 8373, pp. 359–381. Springer, Heidelberg (2014)
10. Lee, E.A.: Cyber physical systems: design challenges. In: 2008 11th IEEE International Symposium on Object Oriented Real-Time Distributed Computing (ISORC), pp. 363–369. IEEE (2008)
11. Mahadevan, N., Dubey, A., Karsai, G.: Application of software health management techniques. In: Proceedings of the 6th International Symposium on Software Engineering for Adaptive and Self-Managing Systems, pp. 1–10. ACM (2011)
12. Object Management Group: Data Distribution Service for Real-time Systems Specification, 1.0 edn., March 2003
13. Object Management Group: Light Weight CORBA Component Model Revised Submission, OMG Document realtime/03-05-05 edn., May 2003
14. Object Management Group: The Common Object Request Broker: Architecture and Specification Version 3.1, Part 3: CORBA Component Model, OMG Document formal/2008-01-08 edn., January 2008
15. OMG: Deployment and Configuration Final Adopted Specification. http://www.omg.org/members/cgi-bin/doc?ptc/03-07-08.pdf
16. Otte, W.R., Dubey, A., Pradhan, S., Patil, P., Gokhale, A., Karsai, G., Willemsen, J.: F6COM: a component model for resource-constrained and dynamic space-based computing environment. In: Proceedings of the 16th IEEE International Symposium on Object-oriented Real-time Distributed Computing (ISORC 2013), Paderborn, Germany, June 2013

17. Otte, W., Gokhale, A., Schmidt, D.: Predictable deployment in component-based enterprise distributed real-time and embedded systems. In: Proceedings of the 14th International ACM Sigsoft Symposium on Component Based Software Engineering, pp. 21–30. ACM (2011)
18. Pradhan, S., Dubey, A., Levendovszky, T., Kumar, P.S., Emfinger, W.A., Balasubramanian, D., Otte, W., Karsai, G.: Achieving resilience in distributed software systems via self-reconfiguration. J. Syst. Softw. (2016)
19. Pradhan, S., Gokhale, A., Otte, W., Karsai, G.: Real-time fault-tolerant deployment and configuration framework for cyber physical systems. In: Proceedings of the Work-in-Progress Session at the 33rd IEEE Real-time Systems Symposium (RTSS 2012). IEEE, San Juan, Puerto Rico, USA, December 2012
20. Salehie, M., Tahvildari, L.: Self-adaptive software: landscape and research challenges. ACM Trans. Auton. Adapt. Syst. (TAAS) 4(2), 14 (2009)

cloud-ATAM: Method for Analysing Resilient Attributes of Cloud-Based Architectures

David Ebo Adjepon-Yamoah[✉]

School of Computing Science, Centre for Software Reliability, Newcastle University,
Newcastle-upon-Tyne NE1 7RU, UK
d.e.adjepon-yamoah@ncl.ac.uk

Abstract. In this work, we argue that the existing architecture evaluation methods have limitations when assessing architectures interfacing with unpredictable environments such as the Cloud. The unpredictability of this environment is attributed to the dynamic elasticity, scale, and continuous evolution of the cloud topology. As a result, architectures interfacing such unpredictable environments are expected to encounter many uncertainties. It is however, important to focus on, and present holistic approaches combining aspects of both dynamic and static analysis of architecture resilience attributes. This paper introduces an ATAM derived methodology - *cloud-ATAM* - for evaluating the *trade-off* between multiple resilience quality attributes (i.e. *availability* and *performance*) of a cloud-based Reactive Architecture for *Global Software Development*.

Keywords: ATAM · Resilient architectures · Cloud computing · GSD

1 Introduction

Service Oriented Architecture (SOA) [1] might be treated as a state of the art approach to the design and implementation of enterprise software, which is driven by business requirements. Within the last decade a number of concepts related to SOA have been developed, including enterprise service bus, web services, design patterns, service orchestration and choreography, and various security standards. Due to the fact that there are many technologies that cover the area of SOA, the development and evaluation of SOA compliant architectures is especially interesting [2]. The buzzing concept of *cloud computing* represents a mix of most of these concepts and hence, serves as a good SOA example.

In this work, we argue that the existing architecture evaluation methods have limitations when assessing architectures interfacing with unpredictable environments such as the Cloud [3]. The cloud environment is fundamentally different from the classical environments for which most software evaluation methods were developed [3,4]. The unpredictability of this environment is attributed to the dynamic elasticity, scale, and continuous evolution of the Cloud topology (e.g. due to new services, mash-ups, unpredictable modes of service use,

© Springer International Publishing Switzerland 2016
I. Crnkovic and E. Troubitsyna (Eds.): SERENE 2016, LNCS 9823, pp. 105–114, 2016.
DOI: 10.1007/978-3-319-45892-2_8

fluctuations in QoS provision due to unpredictable load/growth etc.) [4]. As a result, architectures interfacing such unpredictable environments are expected to encounter many uncertainties. These challenges call for holistic approaches combining aspects of both dynamic and static evaluation. The aim of this research is to present a methodology - *cloud-ATAM* - for evaluating the trade-off between multiple resilience quality attributes of *small-to-medium size* (i.e. ISO/IEC 14143:1998 & COSMIC Full FP 2.2 for classifying system size) architectures in unpredictable environments such as the Cloud. Our approach applies a well established method in software architecture analysis called Architectural Trade-off Analysis Method (ATAM) [5]. ATAM generates a number of outputs such as: a prioritised list of quality attributes, a list of architectural decisions made, a map linking architectural decisions to attributes, lists of risk and non-risks, and lists of sensitivities and trade-offs. In this work, we use the derived *cloud-ATAM* to *design* the Reactive Architecture [6], and to *analyse* the trade-off between the availability and performance attributes. To support the analysis of the Reactive Architecture, *cloud-ATAM* considers a non-trivial set of *scenarios*, and plan to use a particular specialisation of architectural styles called *attribute-based architectural styles* (ABASs) [7]. We answer the research question: *"What is the trade-off between availability and performance quality attributes identified by the cloud-ATAM for the cloud-based Reactive Architecture?"*

2 Background

A brief overview of the ATAM, and ABAS are presented as a precursor for our discussion about the *cloud-ATAM* in the following section.

2.1 Quality Attribute Trade-Off Analysis with ATAM

Architectural analysis is a key practice for organisations that use Software Architectures (SAs). This is essential because SAs are complex and involve many design *trade-offs*, and ensures that *architectural decisions* appropriately mitigate *risks*. The ATAM is considered as a matured and validated scenario-based SA evaluation method [8]. The *inputs* of the ATAM are *scenarios* elicited by stakeholders and documented descriptions of the architecture. The ATAM is typically constituted with nine steps: (1) Present the ATAM, (2) Present the Business Drivers, (3) Present the Architecture, (4) Identify Architectural Approaches, (5) Generate the Quality Attribute Utility Tree, (6) Analyse the Architectural Approaches, (7) Brainstorm and Prioritise Scenarios, (8) Analyse the Architectural Approaches, and (9) Present Results. The goal of the ATAM is to analyse architectural approaches with respect to *scenarios* generated from business drivers for the purpose of identifying *risk points* in the architecture. This is achieved by a disciplined reasoning about SA relating to multiple quality attributes. There are two important classifications of *risk points* namely *sensitivity points* and *trade-off points*. A *sensitivity point* affects the achievement of one quality attribute; a *trade-off point* affects the achievement of more than one quality attributes, where one improves and the other degrades. These

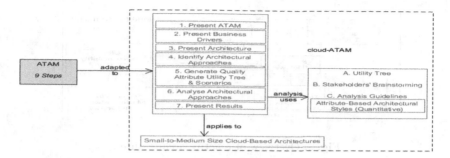

Fig. 1. *cloud-ATAM*: Adapted ATAM with defined 3-step analysis approach

risk points, together with extensive documentations of the architecture, scenarios, and quality-attributes analysis are the *products* of ATAM. The ATAM also explicitly relates architectural risks and trade-offs to business drivers.

2.2 Attribute-Based Architectural Style

An Attribute-Based Architectural Styles (ABASs) [7] is an architectural style in which the constraints focus on component types and patterns of interaction that are particularly relevant to quality attributes. ABASs aid architecture evaluation by focusing the stakeholders' attention on the patterns that dominate the architecture, by suggesting *attribute-specific questions* associated with the style. Such questions are, in turn, inspired by the *attribute characterisations*. Each attribute characterisation is divided into three categories: *external stimuli*, *architectural parameters*, and *responses*. With regards to the *availability* attribute, its *stimuli* are from *source* (i.e. hardware or software faults), and *type* (i.e. value, timing, and stopping). Its *parameters* are the *hardware redundancy*, *software redundancy*, *voting*, *retry*, and *failover*. Finally, the *responses* generated are *availability*, *reliability*, *levels of service*, and *mean time to failure*. Also, the *stimuli* of the *performance* attribute are *mode*, *source*, and *frequency regularity*. The performance *parameters* considered in architectural decisions are mainly *resource* such as *CPUs*, *sensors*, *networks*, *memories*, *actuators*, etc. and *resource arbitration* in the form of *queuing* and *pre-emption*. Finally, the *responses* from the performance characterisation are *latency*, *throughput*, and *precedence*.

3   cloud-ATAM

The *cloud-ATAM* (see Fig. 1) is motivated by the complex and iterative nature of the ATAM even for small-to-medium size architectures (classed with ISO/IEC 14143:1998 & COSMIC Full FP 2.2). Typically, such architectures do not need to undertake all the steps of the ATAM. Due to the size of such projects, some steps can be combined into a new step, and some activities of some steps can be optional. Here, *generating the quality attribute utility tree* process of *Step 5* can be combined with the *prioritising scenarios* process of *Step 7* in ATAM. Also, the *analysing the architectural approaches* process of *Step 6 and 8* are repeated, and can be extended with *noting the impact of scenarios on the architectural*

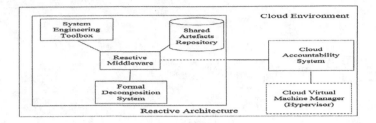

Fig. 2. Overview of reactive architecture

approaches of *Step 8*. These changes are particularly important especially in addressing the perceived weakness of ATAM due to its iterative nature which requires a substantial number of human experts on the team at different times [3]. It is often expensive to speculate the availability of such domain experts for such projects due to budgetary or time constraints [3]. Here, we adapt ATAM into a seven-step methodology. The analysis of the architecture is undertaken in two phases: Phase 1 (Steps 1–5) and Phase 2 (Steps 6–7). Phase 1 is *architect-centric* and concentrates on eliciting and analysing architectural information. Here, the *cloud-ATAM* uses a non-trivial set of *scenarios* to analyse the cloud-based architecture. Phase 2 is *stakeholder-centric* and elicits points of view from a more diverse and larger group of stakeholders, and verifies, and then builds on the results of Phase 1. *cloud-ATAM* presents an *enrichment* in terms of coverage (i.e. unpredictable behaviour) to ATAM in the form of a three-step scenario-based analysis approach: (1) Utility Tree, (2) Stakeholders' Brainstorming, and (3) *guideline* utilising ABAS to *quantitatively* reason about quality attributes.

3.1   Reactive Architecture for *cloud-ATAM* Analysis

The designed set of scenarios is presented based on a Reactive Architecture (RA) [6] (see Fig. 2). The RA is for *global software development* (GSD), where the cloud is the best facilitating environment. This RA is composed of systems such as the Reactive Middleware (RM), the Cloud Accountability System (CAS), the Formal Decomposition System (FDS), the Shared Artefacts Repository (SAR), and the System Engineering Toolbox (SET). These systems are designed as web services (WSs). Web services are necessary to support the deployment and operation on a cloud platform. The RA stands to benefit from the scalability, cost-effectiveness, flexibility, multi-user access, etc. provided by cloud computing. The collective mission of the systems is to facilitate *artefact-driven* and *role-based* support for cloud-based GSD. To this end, the RM which plays a central role in the RA to provide cloud-based services towards *change management* and *traceability* in projects involving distributed teams. The RM aims to assist system engineers to manage changes and trace the cause-and-effect of these changes on artefacts created or used in the various system engineering processes.

4   Evaluating the Reactive Architecture

Here, we analyse the cloud-based Reactive Architecture using the scenario-based *utility tree* approach of the three-step *cloud-ATAM* analysis (see Fig. 1).

Table 1. Mapping requirements to quality attributes of reactive architecture

Attribute Goals	ID	Attribute-Specific Requirements
Operability	O1	The Reactive Architecture must store all artefacts created in the composing systems
	O2*	It must monitor and trace all changes to these artefacts to inform system stakeholders (also P1)
	O3	The System Engineering Toolbox must facilitate sequential and parallel execution of tools in a workflow manner
	O4	The Formal Decomposition System must provided a high capacity and dedicated channel to coordinate real-time analysis on artefacts for local client computers and on remote cloud environment (also P3)
	O5	The Cloud Accountability System must gather dependability metrics from several virtual machines, and perform a synchronous analysis of these metrics
Performance	P1*	It must monitor and trace all changes to these artefacts to inform system stakeholders (also O2)
	P2*	The Reactive Middleware must enable heterogeneous access and analysis operations on artefacts in the Shared Artefacts Repository (also A2)
	P3	The Formal Decomposition System must provided a high capacity and dedicated channel to coordinate real-time analysis on artefacts for local client computers and on remote cloud environment (also O4)
	P4	Security mechanisms must not degrade defined performance threshold. Specifically, response time for create, delete, update, and display artefact/data operations should not exceed 5 s at peak cloud (i.e. architecture) period and less than 1 s during off-peak period (also S1)
	P5	The Reactive Architecture must do all this while meeting the performance and availability requirements to allow it to keep up with the sturdy stream of data and operations on artefacts from the system engineering processes (also A4)
Scalability	Sc1	The Reactive Architecture must support multiple users concurrently
	Sc2*	The Reactive Architecture must provide capacity to scale quickly to accommodate changing demands of system developers, and failures (also A1)
Availability	A1*	The Reactive Architecture must provide capacity to scale quickly to accommodate changing demands of system developers, and failures (also Sc2)
	A2*	The Reactive Middleware must enable heterogeneous access and analysis operations on artefacts in the Shared Artefacts Repository (also P2)
	A3	Critical systems such as the Reactive Middleware must not constitute a single point of failure which will affect the uptime of the system and the architecture (also R1)
	A4	The Reactive Architecture must do all this while meeting the performance and availability requirements to allow it to keep up with the sturdy stream of data and operations on artefacts from the system engineering processes (also P5)
Maintainability	M1	The Shared Artefacts Repository must be backed up asynchronously to facilitate roll-back of repository artefacts
Reliability	R1	Critical systems such as the Reactive Middleware must not constitute a single point of failure which will affect the uptime of the system and the architecture (also A3)
Security	S1	Security mechanisms must not degrade defined performance threshold. Specifically, response time for create, delete, update, and display artefact/data operations should not exceed 5 s at peak cloud (i.e. architecture) period and less than 1 s during off-peak period (also P4)

Table 2. Classified attribute-specific questions

Attribute Specific Questions ID	Attribute Specific Questions
ASQ1	What facilities exist in the software architecture (if any) for self-testing and monitoring of software components? (Availability)
ASQ2	What facilities exist in the software architecture (if any) for redundancy, liveness monitoring, and fail-over? (Availability)
ASQ3	How is data consistency maintained so that one component can take over from another and be sure that it is in a consistent state with the failed component? (Availability)
ASQ4	What is the process and/or task view of the system, including mapping of these processes/tasks to hardware and communication mechanisms between them? (Performance)
ASQ5	What functional dependencies exist among the software components? (Performance)
ASQ6	What data is kept in the database? How big is it, how much does it change, who reads/writes it? (Performance)
ASQ7	How are resources allocated to service requests? (Performance)
ASQ8	What are the anticipated frequency and volume of data transmitted among the system components? (Performance)

4.1 Present the ATAM

The ATAM has been introduced in Sect. 2.1, and *cloud-ATAM* in Sect. 3.

4.2 Present Business Drivers

We briefly present the business drivers (i.e. requirements) of the Reactive Architecture (RA) which cover several quality attributes: operability - [O], performance - [P], scalability - [Sc], availability - [A], maintainability - [M], reliability - [R], and security - [S] (see Table 1). We focus on the *availability* (A1, A2, A3, A4, A5) and *performance* (P1, P2, P3, P4, P5) related requirements.

4.3 Present the Architecture

The Reactive Architecture [6] has been introduced in Sect. 3.1.

4.4 Identify Architectural Approaches

Here, some *attribute-specific questions* (see Table 2) are asked to draw attention to the patterns that dominate the Reactive Architecture. We also identify some *architectural approaches* in Table 3 which inspires the presented questions.

Table 3. Architectural approaches for the reactive architecture

Architectural Approach ID	Architectural Approaches
AD1	We use the component-and-connector architectural style to represent the various components and connections/interfaces of the Reactive Architecture. This is particularly relevant because it expresses the run-time behaviour of the architecture under review. Also, interfaces are defined as application programming interfaces (APIs)
AD2	We avoid the distributed data repository approach in designing the Shared Artefacts Repository. This avoids issues with database consistency and possible modifiability concerns
AD3	The client-server approach is best fit for the data-centric Shared Artefacts Repository system
AD4	The Reactive Middleware will be adequately represented using the client-server approach
AD5	Since the Reactive Middleware and the Shared Artefacts Repository constitute a single point of failure, we present the following approaches:
AD6	- Backup of artefacts in the Shared Artefacts Repository
	- Distributed services for the components of the Reactive Middleware
AD7	Schema-free NoSQL data management system (DMS) is necessary for the Shared Artefacts Repository to minimise or remove bottlenecks
AD8	An independent communication components approach for communication among the Reactive middleware, Shared Artefacts Repository, Cloud Accountability System, and the Formal Decomposition System. Such communication approach is particularly relevant for the distributed components of the Cloud Accountability System

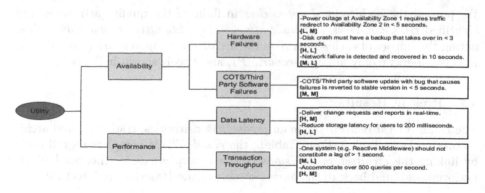

Fig. 3. Attribute utility tree of reactive architecture (adapted from [8])

Table 4. Prioritised quality attribute scenarios (ordered)

No.	Quality Attribute Scenarios	ScenarioID	Numbered Value
1	Disk (i.e. data repository) crash must have a back-up that takes over in less than 3 s	A2	1
2	**Deliver change requests and reports in real-time**	P1	1
3	Reduce storage latency for users to 200 ms	P2	1
4	Accommodate over 500 queries per second	P4	1
5	Network failure is detected and recovered in 10 s	A3	2
6	COTS/Third party software update with bug that causes failures is reverted to stable version in less than 5 s	A4	2
7	One system (e.g. Reactive Middleware) should not constitute a lag greater than 1 s	P3	2
8	Power outage at *Availability Zone 1** requires traffic redirect to *Availability Zone 2** in less than 5 s	A1	3

4.5 Generate the Quality Attribute Utility Tree and Scenarios

At this point, we identify, prioritise, and refine the most important quality attribute goals in a utility tree format (i.e. Fig. 3). We also created *scenarios* that are used to precisely elicit the specific quality goals against which the architecture is analysed. Also, the quality attribute scenarios are prioritised based on (1) *how important they are to the overall mission of the architecture*, and (2) *the perceived difficulty in realising them in the architecture* (see Table 4).

4.6 Analyse the Architectural Approaches

We probed the *architectural approaches* in light of the quality attributes and identified *risks*, *non-risks*, and *trade-offs* using *quality attribute questions*, while noting the impact of each scenario on the *architectural approaches* (see Table 5). In this paper, we only analyse *scenario P1*, and this is shown in Table 6.

4.7 Present Results

The *cloud-ATAM* delivers the main *products*: sensitivities, trade-offs, and architectural risks in Table 5. From Table 6, the *cloud-ATAM* completed a full cycle by linking the *architectural decisions* to the *quality attributes* (i.e. availability, performance), and back to the *business goals* of the Reactive Architecture.

Table 5. Analysis of sensitivities, trade-offs, risks & non-risks for the utility tree

Sensitivities:	* **S1:** Concern over network latency * **S2:** Using a data-centric and client-server approach for the central repository can facilitate data integrity and consistency, but it makes the architecture sensitive to its faults and bottlenecks
	* **S3:** Similarly, the central role played by the Reactive Middleware makes the architecture sensitive to faults, resource (i.e. CPU, memory) malfunctions or unavailability
Trade-offs:	* **T1:** Availability (+) vrs Performance (-) vrs Reliability (-): defining a central artefacts repository makes artefacts readily available, but may be faced with bottlenecks when there are a burst of queries on the repository
	* **T2:** Availability (+) vrs Performance (+): using APIs for component interfaces facilitate readily access to resources, and boosts performance
	* **T3:** Availability (+) vrs Performance (-): client-server approach for the Reactive Middleware allows for multi-client service, but there can be an overwhelming network management performance constraint
	* **T4:** Availability (+) vrs Performance (-) vrs Reliability (+): backing up the artefacts in the primary Shared Artefacts Repository allows for fail-over assurance and increased reliability, but the asynchronous back-up process can affect performance
Risks:	* **R1:** Data integrity
	* **R2:** The risk is that the Reactive Middleware and the Shared Artefacts Repository constitute a single point of failure
Non-Risks:	* **N1:** The non-risk is the use of application programming interface (API) approach which should stay compatible
	* **N2:** The independent communication connections should enable real-time data transfer

Table 6. Analysis of performance scenario - **P1** - (see Table 5 for the description of S1, S2, T1, etc.) and (**C&C + API**: Component-and-connector architectural style and API, **SAR**: Shared Artefacts Repository, **RM**: Reactive Middleware, and **ICC**: Independent Communication Components)

Analysis of Architectural Approach using a Performance-related Scenario				
Scenario ID : *P1*	**Scenario:** *Deliver change requests and reports in real-time*			
Attribute(s)	*Performance (also Availability)*			
Environment	*Normal Operations*			
Stimulus	*Responsiveness to change events*			
Response	*real-time*			
Architectural Decisions	**Sensitivity**	**Trade-off**	**Risk**	**Non-Risk**
AD1 C&C + API	S1			N1
AD2				
AD3 Client-Server SAR	S2	T1	R1, R2	N1
AD4 Client-Server RM	S3	T3	R2	N1
AD5 Back-up	S1,S2	T4		N1
AD6 DS RM	S1		R1	N1
AD7 Schema-free-SAR			R2	
AD8 ICC	S1			N2

5   Conclusion

In this paper, we have motivated the need for architecture evaluation methods suitable for the dynamic unpredictable cloud environments. In particular, we have presented an evaluation method - *cloud-ATAM* - derived from ATAM for evaluating the *availability* and *performance* quality attributes of a cloud-based Reactive Architecture. The results from Tables 5 and 6 indicate that the *cloud-ATAM* found some trade-offs (i.e. T1, T3, T4). This answers our research question, and validates our hypothesis that *the cloud-ATAM is able to identify trade-offs between the availability and performance quality attributes for the Reactive Architecture*. A detailed discussion of the evaluation *products* is limited.

References

1. Josuttis, N.: SOA in Practice: The Art of Distributed System Design. O'Reilly Media Inc., Sebastopol (2007)
2. Szwed, P., Skrzynski, P., Rogus, G., Werewka, J.: Ontology of architectural decisions supporting ATAM based assessment of SOA architectures. In: Federated Conference on Computer Science and Information Systems (FedCSIS), pp. 287–290, September 2013
3. Faniyi, F., Bahsoon, R., Evans, A., Kazman, R.: Evaluating security properties of architectures in unpredictable environments: a case for cloud. In: 2011 9th Working IEEE/IFIP Conference on Software Architecture (WICSA), pp. 127–136, June 2011
4. Ardagna, D.: Cloud, multi-cloud computing: current challenges and future applications. In: 2015 IEEE/ACM 7th International Workshop on Principles of Engineering Service-Oriented and Cloud Systems (PESOS), pp. 1–2, May 2015
5. Kazman, R., Klein, M., Clements, P., Compton, N.L., Col, L.: ATAM: Method for Architecture Evaluation (2000)
6. Adjepon-Yamoah, D., Romanovsky, A., Iliasov, A.: A reactive architecture for cloud-based system engineering. In: Proceedings of the 2015 International Conference on Software, System Process, ICSSP 2015, Tallinn, Estonia, pp. 77–81. ACM (2011)
7. Klein, M., Kazman, R., Bass, L., Carriere, J., Barbacci, M., Lipson, H.: Attribute-based architecture styles. In: Donohoe, P. (ed.) Software Architecture. IFIP, vol. 12, pp. 225–243. Springer, New York (1999)
8. Clements, P., Kazman, R., Klein, M.: Evaluating Software Architectures: Methods and Case Studies. Addison-Wesley Longman Publishing Co., Inc., Boston (2002)

Testing

Automated Test Case Generation for the CTRL Programming Language Using Pex: Lessons Learned

Stefan Klikovits[1,2]([✉]), David P.Y. Lawrence[1], Manuel Gonzalez-Berges[2], and Didier Buchs[1]

[1] Centre Universitaire d'Informatique, Université de Genève, Carouge, Switzerland
{stefan.klikovits,david.lawrence,didier.buchs}@unige.ch
[2] CERN, European Organization for Nuclear Research, Geneva, Switzerland
{stefan.klikovits,manuel.gonzalez}@cern.ch

Abstract. Over the last decade code-based test case generation techniques such as combinatorial testing or dynamic symbolic execution have seen growing research popularity. Most algorithms and tool implementations are based on finding assignments for input parameter values in order to maximise the execution branch coverage. In this paper we first present ITEC, a tool for automated test case generation in CTRL, as well as initial results of test cases executions on one of CERN's SCADA frameworks. Our tool relies on Microsoft's Pex for its code exploration. For the purpose of using this existing test generation tool, we have to translate the proprietary CTRL code into C#, one of Pex's operating languages. Our main contribution lies in detailing a formal foundation for this step through source code decomposition and anonymization. We then propose a quality measure that is used to determine our confidence into the translation and the generated test cases.

Keywords: Automated test case generation · Resilience · Software testing · Translation validation · Execution environment resilience

1 Introduction

At the Large Hadron Collider (LHC), its experiments and several other installations at CERN physicists and engineers employ a Supervisory Control And Data Acquisition (SCADA) system to mediate between operators and controllers/frontend computers which connect to the sensors and actuators. As such applications require hundreds of controllers to be configured, CERN has developed two frameworks on top of Siemens' *Simatic WinCC Open Architecture* (WinCC OA) [4] SCADA platform to facilitate their creation.

Due to lack of tool support for the WinCC OA's scripting language Control (CTRL) [5], it was so far not possible to write and execute unit tests in an efficient manner. Recently CERN started the development of such a unit testing framework to fill this need. However, after more than ten years of development,

© Springer International Publishing Switzerland 2016
I. Crnkovic and E. Troubitsyna (Eds.): SERENE 2016, LNCS 9823, pp. 117–132, 2016.
DOI: 10.1007/978-3-319-45892-2_9

CERN is left with over 500,000 lines of CTRL code for which only a very small set of unit tests exist. Hence, the verification of the source code remains a mainly manual task leading to high testing costs in terms of manpower and slower release times.

This situation is especially tedious during the frequent changes in the WinCC OA execution environment. Before every introduction of a new operating system version, the installation of patches or the release of a new framework version the code base needs to be re-tested. Over the lifetime of the LHC, these environment changes happen repeatedly (often annually) and involve a major testing overhead. To overcome this issue, we decided to look into automatic test case generation. Since no tool exists that natively supports CTRL code we faced the choice between two solutions: 1. Develop an automatic test case generation tool specifically for CTRL; 2. Translate the CTRL code into the operating language of an existing automatic test case generation tool.

In order to reuse the theoretical knowledge gained over the years by established tools, we chose to translate CTRL code to C# in order to use Microsoft Research's Pex tool [11], a program that performs test case generation through dynamic symbolic execution [3]. To support this solution, we developed a tool called *Iterative TEst Case* system (ITEC). This tool helped to build up regression tests that can then be reused on the evolving system to ensure its quality. ITEC works on the assumption that the current system reached a stable state after 13 years of continuous use.

After finishing the first version of the tool, we applied it on a large part of the CTRL code base at CERN and had initial execution results. Based on this, we are now able to cast a critical eye over the quality of our approach.

The cornerstone of the chosen solution is the translation from CTRL to C# in order to use Pex. Evidently, if this translation is erroneous, the generated test cases would not be trustworthy. To ensure the quality of our approach, we must be able to validate the translation.

In this paper, we will shortly introduce how ITEC works and show first execution results. Based on these results and our experience, we will mainly focus on the validation of the translation from CTRL code to C#. Finally, we will discuss the translation and test quality metrics that take our translation validity study into consideration.

This paper is structured as follows: Sect. 2 discusses of the related work in terms of language translations and their verification, Sect. 3 presents an overview of ITEC and its individual components, Sect. 4 shows our execution results on one of the frameworks used in production, Sect. 5 presents our methodology to verify our language translation, addressing first general concepts before diving into the applied translation from CTRL to C#, Sect. 6 discusses a metric to express the overall quality of the tests based on coverage metrics, finally Sect. 7 gives an outlook on future work and concludes.

2   Related Work

As the main contribution of this paper lies in the verification of translation validity, we address in this section related works on this subject. Due to spacial constraints and the large amount of research in this field, we will however not be able to give an exhaustive description of all related works, but instead select the ones that are most closely related to our works.

The translation of CTRL code falls into the domain of source-to-source compilers or transpilers. The field of compiler verification has been extensively studied for compilations from high-level to low-level languages, including optimizing compilers using formal correctness proofs for the compiler software. An alternative approach introduced by [13] and extended by [12,15] is called translation validation. These works are based on the idea to check the translation output for equivalence to the input, rather than the compiler itself.

Since the translation is based on the abstract syntax tree (AST) that we obtain from parsing CTRL, the translation can also be seen as a model transformation. While many approaches to validation of model transformations have been proposed, we found the white box approach to validation of model transformation given in [9] of interest for our cases, as the authors argue for the use of large sets of generated test cases to perform validation. [6] introduces a test adequacy criterion for model transformations of the model driven architecture. They discuss partitioning and the choice of representative values as a means to gain trust in the model transformation program. Although their example is based on UML models, we see their approach as a general enough for our code translation purposes.

Another approach treats the translation as specific generation of code from an AST. The design, creation and also validation of code generators has been extensively discussed in [7], where a detailed overview on the topic of testing of code generators is given.

3   Tool Description

There exist different approaches to automatic test case generation and a lot of tools have been implemented for various programming languages. Unfortunately, none of these tools natively supports CTRL code with all its particularities, such as implicit castings, special data types and reference parameters. When facing the choice whether it was preferable to implement our own automated test case generation (ATCG) tool for CTRL or to adapt our code to be able to use an existing tool, we chose the latter solution in order to build upon the experience and the knowledge others earned through the years. CTRL's language specificities led us in choosing Microsoft's Pex tool and the underlying C# language. Amongst the other options, this one seems to be the most flexible in terms of language constructs and supports. Furthermore, C# and CTRL are similar in many points, reducing the effort required to translate the code.

In the following subsections we will give a brief overview of the ITEC workflow, depicted in Fig. 1.

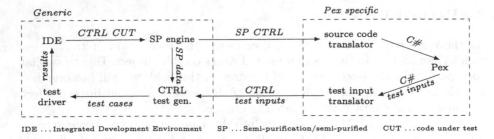

Fig. 1. ITEC workflow. The figure depicts ITEC's components (nodes) and the information passed between them (arrows). The dashed boxes separate the components logically into two types: generic and Pex-specific components.

3.1 Semi-purification and CUT Isolation

The first step is the isolation of code under test (CUT). Code dependencies such as function calls other CTRL routines, accesses to global variables or data stored in a database complicate the testing process.

In order to effectively generate unit test cases, we have to remove these dependencies and replace them with predefined values. For this purpose we use semi-purification [8], an approach where dependencies are replaced by additional input parameters to the CUT. The values generated for the new parameters will then be used to specify test doubles for the test execution.

3.2 Translation

The semi-purified code is then translated to the ATCG tool's operating language – in our case this is C#. The translation process is non-trivial, as statements and constructs need to be mapped from one language to another.

To mention two examples for which the translation required adaptations: 1. C# does not allow indexers (index references to list elements) to be passed as reference parameters; 2. CTRL variables are automatically initialized with a default value, while C# requires explicit initialization. Additionally we manually implemented most of the built-in CTRL standard library, including missing data types in C#. More details on the translation validity will be given in Sect. 5.

3.3 ATCG Execution

Following the translation, the C# code is combined with the manually translated artefacts and the parameterized unit test (PUT). The PUT can be thought of as a parameterized routine that executes the CUT and subsequently performs assertions. PUTs are not Pex-specific but can be found in many modern unit testing frameworks such as JUnit, NUnit and others.

After the compilation of these resources, the ATCG tool (Pex) is triggered.

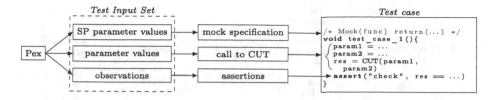

Fig. 2. Test case generation from Pex output

3.4 Test Case Creation

In this phase, the values from the generated test input sets are re-translated into CTRL. The next step is to use the semi-purification knowledge to separate the Pex-produced values into CUT parameters, parameters added by semi-purification and other observations. Depending on the category, the values are used for different parts of the test case. Figure 2 shows the three categories of values that Pex produces and their transformation to code. It is to be said, that since CTRL does not support reflection natively, mock specifications have to be transformed into mock functions at execution time.

3.5 TC Execution, Mock Generation

At test run time, the mock specifications (see Fig. 2) are used to create function doubles which simulate the dependencies' expected behaviour. The current version of mock specifications are fairly simple, but an extension has been proposed to allow for more complex behaviour (different behaviour based on timing, iterations, etc.). Function doubles replace dependencies during test execution and return predefined values. They can also perform some simple assertions, if specified.

4 Results

To test the effectiveness of ITEC we executed it on 1111 functions found in JCOP [2], one of CERN's two WinCC OA frameworks. The test case generation was performed with eight concurrent threads on a Windows 7 virtual machine with eight CPUs (each 2.4 GHz) and 16 GB RAM. The generation and execution of test cases had a time out of two and one minute, respectively. We ended up with 602 functions that were successfully translated to C# and used for test input generation.

The remaining 509 functions were not translated due to the following reasons (texts in brackets provide references in Fig. 3): 166 contained unsupported features or functions (*Unsupported*), 159 could not be translated due to unavailable dependencies (*SP Err*), 184 invalid translations (*Translation Err*) that led to compilation errors.

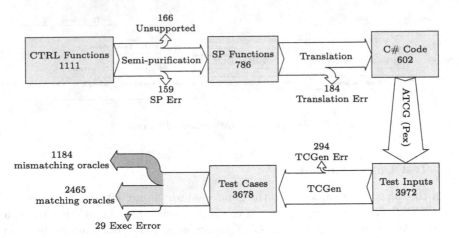

Fig. 3. Sankey diagram, displaying the quantitative analysis of the execution on a subset of the JCOP framework

For the 602 successful translated functions Pex produced 3972 test inputs. During translation of these inputs to CTRL, filtering of invalid and untranslatable input removed 294 errors (*TCGen Err*), leaving 3678 implemented CTRL test cases.

An analysis of the test case executions showed that 2465 test cases had a matching between CTRL execution result and Pex' predictions, whereas 1184 did not (no match between CTRL and Pex execution), 29 test cases crashed during execution.

We further analysed the code coverage of the respective CUTs using WinCC OA's built-in line coverage reporting. Table 1 shows the number of functions grouped by their line coverage. The first column displays the coverage ranges, the second column shows the number of functions with that coverage when executing all test cases and the third column the number of functions when only taking test cases with matching oracles into account.

The first row of the table indicates that over a third of the functions reach 100 % code coverage, both with all test cases and when only taking test cases with matching oracles into account. In general the coverage of relatively few functions drops due to restricting the coverage calculation to only test cases with matching oracles. However, one thing is clearly noticeable. In total, there are only 15 functions with 0 % coverage, meaning that there exist no tests at all for these functions. The reason for this could be that either no test inputs were generated, due to too complex constraints, or that only invalid test inputs were created which could not be translated to CTRL. When only looking at matching oracle test cases this number grows to 51, indicating that there are 36 functions that only have test cases which mismatch the expected results.

It seems though that Pex works well to achieve high code coverage (56 % of the functions have ≥ 75% line coverage).

Table 1. Code (line) coverage: all test cases and test cases with matching results only and total

Line coverage	# Functions (all TCs)	# Functions (with matching oracle)
100 %	230 (38 %)	215 (36 %)
75 % - 99	129 (21 %)	120 (20 %)
50 % - 74 %	110 (18 %)	111 (18 %)
1 % - 49 %	118 (20 %)	105 (17 %)
0 %	15 (2 %)	51 (8 %)

It should be noted that even though the number of test cases with mismatching results between CTRL and C# is high, the effort put into their generation is not wasted. One can easily see that automatically updating the expected outcome of the test cases could produce a powerful regression test suite. Clearly, our translation from CTRL to C# is not entirely correct, as we would not have test cases with mismatching oracles otherwise.

We did however also identify several caveats. Firstly, producing "sensible" input data seems to be a difficult task for the generation tool (Pex). In our case it would have been beneficial to have Pex produce a list of strings with certain format. Even though theoretically Pex is capable of doing this, the processing time increases dramatically as a result and in many cases the added constraints on the produced data lead to a very low number of test cases and coverage. The execution cost in terms of time and memory grows exponentially with the number of constraints.

Another problem is that Pex's working principle is based on block coverage. This means that Pex will try to procude the smallest set of inputs to cover the CUT. However, this also includes that boundary values or mutation considerations are not taken into account. This results in testsuites that verify the corresponding outcome (same input produces same output) but not the negative cases (changed CUT leads to failing tests).

5 Translation Validation

At the time of writing, the translation from CTRL to C# has not yet been formally verified. In fact, the translation to the ATCG tool's (Pex') operating language represents an essential step in the workflow of our test case generation system. It seems self-evident that an erroneous translation from CTRL to C# would not only lead to a misguided exploration but also invalidate the produced test cases and results. Hence, a validation is required. Unfortunately Siemens does not provide a clear semantic for the CTRL language. For that reason, proofs cannot be utilized to show the validity of our translation.

In this section we will show how to verify a translation from one language to another, using testing and decomposition.

5.1 Syntactical Translation

To start, we need to clearly define the meaning of code translation from a source language to a target language.

Definition 1 (Syntactical translation of a source code in a language to another language). *A syntactical translation is a partial function* $st : L_{src} \to L_{dst}$ *that takes a piece of code* c_1 *written in a source language* L_{src}, $c_1 \in L_{src}$, *and translates it to a piece of code* c_2 *written in a destination language* L_{dst}, $c_2 \in L_{dst}$:

$$c_2 = st(c_1), c_1 \in L_{src} \text{ and } c_2 \in L_{dst} \tag{1}$$

Note that this translation is purely syntactic. Although the translation aims to preserve the code's semantics, the definition above does not take this equivalence into account.

Our next goal is therefore to show this syntactical translation validity. Conceptually, we would like to show an equivalence between the source code and the destination code. However, we cannot show this equivalence in the syntactical domain.

5.2 Semantic Equivalence

We must therefore observe the semantic, denoted with the symbol $[\![.]\!]$ in the following definitions, of each piece of code in their respective language.

Definition 2 (Semantic of source and destination code). *Given a code* c_1 *written in the language* L_{src}, *its execution with a given parameter interpretation* σ *is denoted as:*

$$[\![c_1]\!]^{\sigma}_{L_{src}} = f_{src} \tag{2}$$

$$f_{src} : dom_{L_{src}} \times ... \times dom_{L_{src}} \to dom_{L_{src}} \tag{3}$$

Similarly, for a code c_2 *written in the language* L_{dst}, *its execution with a given parameter interpretation* σ' *is denoted as:*

$$[\![c_2]\!]^{\sigma}_{L_{dst}} = f_{dst} \tag{4}$$

$$f_{dst} : dom_{L_{dst}} \times ... \times dom_{L_{dst}} \to dom_{L_{dst}} \tag{5}$$

To show the semantic equivalence of two codes c_1 and c_2 in their respective languages L_{src} and L_{dst}, we must also be able to map the data types defined in both languages. This mapping defines a relationship between values of equivalent domains in both languages.

Definition 3 (L_{src} and L_{dst} domains mapping). *There exists a partial function* h *such that it maps a variable value defined in the language* L_{src} *to a variable value defined in the language* L_{dst}:

$$h : dom_{L_{src}} \to dom_{L_{dst}} \tag{6}$$

To ease the definition of the partial function H that applies the mapping for all parameters of a given function, we first define the parameters themselves in both domains:

$$dom_{L_{src}} \times ... \times dom_{L_{src}} \in P_{L_{src}} \tag{7}$$

$$dom_{L_{dst}} \times ... \times dom_{L_{dst}} \in P_{L_{dst}} \tag{8}$$

Now we can define the partial function H over these parameters:

$$H : dom_{L_{src}} \times ... \times dom_{L_{src}} \rightarrow dom_{L_{dst}} \times ... \times dom_{L_{dst}} \tag{9}$$

Given the parameters p_{src}, the semantic of H is the following:

$$p_{src} \in dom_{L_{src}} \times ... \times dom_{L_{src}} \tag{10}$$

$$H(p_{src}) = \langle h(p_i)|p_i \in p_{src}, 0 \leq i \leq |p_{src}|\rangle \tag{11}$$

To introduce the translation validity, let's first consider the picture depicted on Fig. 4. Three main parts can be distinguished on this picture.

- The top arrow leading from c_1 to c_2 depicts the translation st of the code c_1 written with the language L_{src} to the code c_2 written in L_{dst};
- The second arrow shows the domains mapping H between L_{src} and L_{dst}. This mapping is used to adapt values chosen for the interpretation σ in dom_{src} to the interpretation made in dom_{dst};
- Finally, the bottom arrow shows the wanted equality between the execution of the code c_1 and c_2.

Formally, we could define this semantic equivalence with the Definition 4.

Definition 4 (Semantic equality).

$$h([\![c_1]\!]_{L_{src}}^{\sigma}) = [\![c_2]\!]_{L_{dst}}^{\sigma'}, \forall \sigma, \forall c_1 \in L_{src}, c_2 = st(c_1) \in L_{dst}, \sigma' = H(\sigma) \tag{12}$$

Take note that in order to define the translation correctness, one must consider all possible codes c_1 written in the language L_{src} and all possible parameter interpretations σ.

Although it is theoretically correct, this is impractical. In fact, constructs or data types of the source language might not be translatable to the destination language. If we take a step back to Definition 1, the syntactical translation is

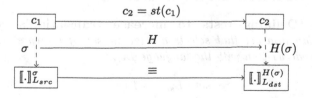

Fig. 4. High level picture of the translation validity

defined as a partial function for this reason. In our translation, we did not find any construct that cannot be translated from CTRL to C#. However, in some cases, the translation can be really arduous and could easily lead to translation errors.

Furthermore, the domains mapping functions h/H are also partial functions (Definition 3). In fact, some data types of the language L_{src} might not be mappable to types in L_{dst}. In our translation, we came across the data type *shape* that is virtually impossible to translate to C#, as illustrated in Example 1.

Example 1 (Domains not existing or not translatable). CTRL provides the data type **shape**. Shapes are pointers to graphics elements, that are used to display information in user interface panels. Which element is pointed to is identified by the graphical object's name. As these names can be set and modified at runtime, it is impossible to know the shape's type, state and attributes.

Based on the previous remarks, proving the validity is close to impossible, especially since a full mapping between the source and the destination languages might not exist. Dániel Várro et al. discuss on that matter when considering model transformation verification in [14]. He mentioned two main concepts as requirements to verify model transformation:

1. *Syntactic completeness*: the source language covers the destination language in terms of constructs;
2. *Syntactic correctness*: the translation leads to a syntactical correct model.

In our case, both requirements can be violated. In fact, one can violate syntactic completeness if the source language does not cover the destination language, as it is the case with the data type *shape* for example. We can however argue that this requirement can be satisfied since both languages are Turing-complete, yet it would be very arduous to do so. As for syntactic correctness, this can be violated due to an erroneous translation that leads to a code that is syntactical incorrect. Furthermore, combinatorial explosion threatens to quickly become a problem if we assume that we need to exercise all possible codes with all input combinations to verify our translation.

5.3   Testing to Increase Confidence

However, we can still increase our confidence in the translation using both testing and the execution of the source code as an oracle.

Definition 5 (Defining tests to increase translation's confidence). *Assuming a function sel that selects a relevant set of interpretations σ for a given source code written with the language L_{src}:*

$$sel : L_{src} \rightarrow \mathcal{P}(\sigma) \tag{13}$$

To increase our confidence in the translation, we need to show that for all chosen interpretations $sel(c_1)$ the execution of both source and destination code are equal, given the domains mapping h/H.

$$h(\llbracket c_1 \rrbracket^{\sigma}_{L_{src}}) = \llbracket st(c_1) \rrbracket^{H(\sigma)}_{L_{dst}}, \forall \sigma \in sel(c_1), c_1 \in L_{src} \tag{14}$$

Note that the selection methodology implemented by the function *sel* is crucial to increase our confidence in the translation, yet we will not address this matter in this paper. We could mention test input generation techniques such anti-random [10] for example or selection hypothesis such as [1] that address the selection of a relevant set of test inputs. For the sake of the argument, we will assume that the methodology chosen is of the greatest quality.

According to our current definition, we must generate tests every time we translate a new source code. Even if this technique works, one can understand that this is a labour intensive activity. Hence, we are now able to increase our confidence in the translation for a source code that satisfies the two requirements previously mentioned, even though it is still cumbersome.

One can make a reasonable assumption saying that the overall semantic of a function is given by the composition of the semantic of its basic block. For that purpose, we assume that no compiler optimizations are applied in order to keep the current structure of the code and satisfy our previous assumption. This assumption eases the overall verification of the translation. In fact, we don't have to check every piece of source code to ensure the quality of our translation, but only to check basic blocks.

Let us now formally define how to verify basic blocks for the translation.

Definition 6 (Structure of a piece of code). *In our case, a piece of code c_1 written in the language L_{src} is a function. This function can be decomposed in a signature sig and a block of statements body:*

$$c_1 = \langle sig, body \rangle \text{ with } c_1 \in L_{src} \tag{15}$$

The body itself is composed of either control blocks, i.e. loop and conditional blocks, or statements:

$$
\begin{aligned}
&body \subseteq \mathcal{P}(block) \\
&stmt : statement \rightarrow block \\
&ift : statement \times block \rightarrow block \\
&while : statement \times block \rightarrow block
\end{aligned} \tag{16}
$$

Note that block is part of the source language:

$$block \in L_{src} \tag{17}$$

From this code structure, we can therefore decompose a source code into its basic blocks.

Definition 7 (Decomposing a source code in basic blocks). *To be able to decompose a source code, we need first to define how to decompose basic blocks.*

$$dec : block \rightarrow \mathcal{P}(statement) \tag{18}$$

$$dec(stmt(stmt1)) = \{stmt1\}$$
$$dec(ift(stmt1, block1)) = stmt1 \cup dec(block1) \tag{19}$$
$$dec(while(stmt1, block1)) = stmt1 \cup dec(block1)$$

The overall decomposition of a source code is therefore given by:

$$decomposition : L_{src} \rightarrow \mathcal{P}(statement)$$
$$decomposition(\langle sig, body \rangle) = \bigcup_{\forall block \in body} dec(block) \tag{20}$$

Furthermore, we generalize the later decomposition by anonymizing variables and constants in statements to only preserve data types. The following example should clarify the decomposition with anonymization:

Example 2 (Decomposition of a source code c_1). Considering the following code c_1:

Listing 1. Example code for decomposition

```
void func(int abc) {
  abc = abc + 1;
  if (abc == 2) {
    abc = 10;
  }
}
```

The decomposition with anonymization of the example code into basic blocks leads to the following result:

$$anonymize(decomposition(c_1)) = anonymize($$
$$dec(stmt(abc = abc + 1))$$
$$\cup \ dec(ift(stmt(abc == 2), stmt(abc = 10))))$$

$$anonymize(decomposition(c_1)) = \{int = int + int, int == int, int = int\} \tag{21}$$

Based on this source code decomposition, we are able to know the anonymized statements that are executed and we can therefore generate tests for each of these statements independently.

Definition 8 (Verifying translation semantic by testing it on basic blocks). *As we were previously addressing tests selection over a whole function, one can therefore define a new selection function addressing only anonymized statements:*

$$sel_{stmt} : stmt \rightarrow \mathcal{P}(\sigma) \tag{22}$$

The set of statements of a given source code c_1 that must be verified is:

$$stmts = anonymize(decomposition(c_1)), c_1 \in L_{src} \qquad (23)$$

One can now redefine the semantic equivalence required for the translation over all statements from the source code c_1 with domains mapping h/H:

$$h([\![stmt]\!]_{L_{src}}^{\sigma}) = [\![st(stmt)]\!]_{L_{dst}}^{H(\sigma)}, \forall stmt \in stmts, \forall \sigma \in sel_{stmt}(stmt) \qquad (24)$$

As we discussed before, this verification can be partial if we have syntactical incompleteness between our languages. However, we can ensure the quality of the translation up to a certain level. We will discuss of that matter in the next section.

6   Quality Metric

Based on the process described in Sect. 5, we base our confidence of a CUT on the validity of its individual statements' translations. We must therefore take them into consideration when addressing tests generation results. In fact, we cannot pragmatically consider that a code coverage of 100 % is trustable if none of the individual statement translations have been verified.

For that purpose, we define a quality metric ϕ that represents our confidence in the translation and its correctness.

Definition 9 (Correctness confidence measure for code). *Given a piece of code c written in a given language L, the function ϕ represents the correctness confidence as a boolean value defining that the code for the translation is tested (1) or not (0).*

$$\phi : L \to \mathcal{B} \qquad (25)$$

This means that for individual statements ϕ denotes whether the basic blocks have been tested or not, as defined in the previous section.

Based on a confidence of a (CUT's) basic block's individual confidence measures, we then define our confidence into the composition of blocks (such as a function) as follows:

Definition 10 (Correctness confidence of a composition). *Let c_1 be a code under test. Let further stmts be the body of the function, consisting of individual statements $stmt_1, \ldots, stmt_n$. We define that our confidence in the entire code as the mean average of the anonymized statements' correctness confidence.*

$$\phi(c_1) = \frac{\sum_{i=1}^{n} \phi(anon_i)}{n}, anon_i \in anons \qquad (26)$$

where anons is $\{anonymize(stmt_1), \ldots, anonymize(stmt_n)\}$, the set of anonymized statements occurring in c_1.

In a case where multiple statements have the same anonymous representation (e.g. multiple integer additions), only one of them is chosen for the calculation. This is to avoid repeated statements or loops to influence the measure.

We then further define our confidence into the correctness of an individual testcase execution.

Definition 11 (Confidence in test case results). *Let tc be a test case using input interpretation σ that executes the code under test c_1. Let stmts be the statements $stmt_1, \ldots, stmt_n$ of c_1. We define our confidence in the correctness of a result obtained by executing tc as the product of the confidence values of the executed statements denoted as $stmts|_\sigma$.*

$$\phi_{tests} : L_{src} \times dom_{src} \times \ldots \times dom_{src} \to \mathcal{B} \qquad (27)$$

$$\phi_{tests}(c_1, \sigma) = \prod_{\forall stmt_i \in stmts|_\sigma} \phi(anonymize(stmt_i)) \qquad (28)$$

Note that for test case executions, the confidence calculation of every statement is taken into account, even if multiple statements have the same anonymization. For repeated execution of the same statement, such as in a loop, every execution is taken into account. This is possible, since the usage of coverage measures provides the execution count for each individual statement.

6.1   Example Calculation of Correctness Confidence

Listing 2 displays a function for which we want to calculate the correctness confidence and Listing 3 shows this function with anonymized statements. For this example we will assume that the anonymized functions $int + +$, $int + int$, $int = int + int$, have been fully tested ($\phi = 1$), while $int > int$ and $int\%int$ have not been validated ($\phi = 0$).

First we will calculate the correctness confidence for the entire translated function. According to Definition 10 we will calculate the mean of the individual types of anonymized statements. For our example, we therefore will end up with the following calculation (subscript texts indicate the line numbers).

$$\phi(func) = \frac{1_{L2} + 1_{L4} + 0_{L5} + 0_{L6}}{4} = 0.5 \qquad (29)$$

Assuming the existence of a passing test case tc that would assert that the result of $func(x, y)$ with $\sigma = \langle 3, 5 \rangle$ is 8, we would calculate its correctness confidence as follows:

$$\phi(func, \sigma) = 1_{L2} * 1_{L3} * 1_{L4} * 0_{L5} * 1_{L8} = 0 \qquad (30)$$

Listing 2. Example function

```
1   int func(int a, int b) {
2       a++
3       a++
4       b = b+2
5       if(a > b){
6           return a
7       } else {
8           return a + b
9       }
10  }
```

Listing 3. Anonymized function

```
1   int func(int, int){
2       int++
3       int++
4       int = int + int
5       if(int > int) {
6           return int
7       } else {
8           return int + int
9       }
10  }
```

7 Conclusion and Future Work

This paper presents the lessons learned during the creation and the execution of our tool, ITEC.

First, we shortly describe ITEC's workflow and the individual steps that are taken for the test cases generation. Based on this, we present our initial results of the test case generation and execution for one of CERN's CTRL frameworks (more than 1000 individual functions). We realize from these results that we could obtain test cases with mismatching oracles when executing equivalent CTRL and C# codes individually with similar inputs. These results outline possible problems in the translation of CTRL code to C#.

To address this issue, we present formal foundations on the validation of the CTRL to C# translation in order to increase our confidence in the chosen approach. Finally, we discuss of a quality measure that allows us to determine the confidence we put into our translations and hence further into our generated test cases.

Based on the work done so far, we aim to extend this research into several areas: 1. Build an extensive test suite of translation validations for basic blocks, and empirically compare the quality metric's predictions with real data; 2. Improve the translation, both to and from C#, to generate fewer failing test cases; 3. Research into ways to improve test case generation in presence of complex constraints, such as input data matching domain formats; 4. Verify the test cases' effectiveness by systematically executing them on mutated versions of the CUT; 5. Study and introduce a way to make these generated regression tests evolve with time as the code is changing.

References

1. Bernot, G., Gaudel, M., Marre, B.: Software testing based on formal specifications: a theory and a tool. Softw. Eng. J. **6**(6), 387–405 (1991). http://ieeexplore.ieee.org/xpl/articleDetails.jsp?arnumber=120426
2. CERN: The JCOP Framework, August 2014. https://j2eeps.cern.ch/wikis/display/EN/JCOP+Framework
3. Csallner, C., Tillmann, N., Smaragdakis, Y.: DySy: dynamic symbolic execution for invariant inference. In: Proceedings of the 30th International Conference on Software Engineering, ICSE 2008, pp. 281–290. ACM, New York (2008). http://doi.acm.org/10.1145/1368088.1368127

4. ETM Professional Control: WinCC OA at a glance. Siemens AG (2012)
5. ETM Professional Control: Control script language (2015). http://etm.at/index.
   e.asp?id=2&sb1=54&sb2=118&sb3=&sname=&sid=&seite_id=118
6. Fleurey, F., Steel, J., Baudry, B.: Validation in model-driven engineering: testing
   model transformations. In: First International Workshop on Model, Design and
   Validation, Proceedings, pp. 29–40, November 2004
7. Jörges, S. (ed.): Construction and Evolution of Code Generators. LNCS, vol. 7747,
   pp. 207–213. Springer, Heidelberg (2013)
8. Klikovits, S., Lawrence, D.P.Y., Gonzalez-Berges, M., Buchs, D.: Considering execution environment resilience: a white-box approach. In: Fantechi, A., Pelliccione,
   P. (eds.) SERENE 2015. LNCS, vol. 9274, pp. 46–61. Springer, Heidelberg (2015)
9. Küster, J.M., Abd-El-Razik, M.: Validation of model transformations – first expe-
   riences using a white box approach. In: Kühne, T. (ed.) MoDELS 2006. LNCS,
   vol. 4364, pp. 193–204. Springer, Heidelberg (2007). http://dx.doi.org/10.1007/
   978-3-540-69489-2_24
10. Malaiya, Y.K.: Antirandom testing: getting the most out of black-box testing. In:
    Sixth International Symposium on Software Reliability Engineering, ISSRE 1995,
    Toulouse, France, 24–27 October 1995, pp. 86–95. IEEE (1995). http://dx.doi.org/
    10.1109/ISSRE.1995.497647
11. Microsoft Research: Pex, Automated White box Testing for .NET. http://research.
    microsoft.com/en-us/projects/pex/
12. Pnueli, A., Siegel, M.D., Singerman, E.: Translation validation. In: Steffen, B. (ed.)
    TACAS 1998. LNCS, vol. 1384, pp. 151–166. Springer, Heidelberg (1998)
13. Samet, H.: Automatically proving the correctness of translations involving opti-
    mized code. Memo AIM, Stanford University (1975). https://books.google.ch/
    books?id=1sI-AAAAIAAJ
14. Varró, D., Pataricza, A.: Automated formal verification of model transformations.
    In: Jürjens, J., Rumpe, B., France, R., Fernandez, E.B. (eds.) CSDUML 2003:
    Critical Systems Development in UML; Proceedings of the UML 2003 Workshop,
    pp. 63–78. No. TUM-I0323 in Technical report, Technische Universitüt München,
    Technische Universität München, September 2003. http://www.inf.mit.bme.hu/
    FTSRG/Publications/varro/2003/csduml2003_vp.pdf
15. Zuck, L.D., Pnueli, A., Goldberg, B.: VOC: a methodology for the translation
    validation of optimizing compilers. J. UCS **9**(3), 223–247 (2003). http://dx.doi.
    org/10.3217/jucs-009-03-0223

A/B Testing in E-commerce Sales Processes

Kostantinos Koukouvis, Roberto Alcañiz Cubero, and Patrizio Pelliccione[✉]

Chalmers University of Technology, University of Gothenburg, Gothenburg, Sweden
patrizio.pelliccione@gu.se

Abstract. E-commerce has traditionally been a field where online controlled experiments, such as A/B testing, take place. Most of these experiments focus on evaluating the front-end of the application and specifically different visual aspects, e.g. creating variations of the layouts, fonts, colors of the site, etc. In this paper we want to experiment whether A/B testing can be used to evaluate e-commerce sales processes and to improve the resilience of these processes. To achieve this goal we developed a tool in collaboration with a company, called Sonician AB, which is focused on marketing automation. The tool has been designed to empower business owners with a virtual assistant able to help customers understanding their needs and making decisions while purchasing products or services. The tool has been evaluated within the company and instantiated in two different business flow cases. Two experiments under real-life conditions show promising results. The paper concludes with lessons learned and a set of guidelines designed to help companies with interest of conducting similar experiments.

1 Introduction

The world-wide-web has evolved to being the perfect playground for evaluating different ideas through controlled experiments. This type of experiments can be called by different names with only slight differences between them, such as randomized experiments, A/B tests, split tests, Control/Treatment tests, MultiVariable Tests (MVT) and parallel flights. One of the earliest examples of running an online A/B test was an experiment carried by Linden[1]. The controlled experiments embody the best scientific design for establishing a causal relationship between changes and their influence on user-observable behavior [10]. In the context of online experimentation, A/B testing can be utilized in order to analyse user behaviour. The idea behind A/B testing in an online environment is to create two variants of a single website and then randomly assigning to each visiting user one of the variants. Those variants are usually called (i) *the control*, which is usually the currently existing version, and (ii) *the treatment*, which is usually a new version that needs to be evaluated.

The variants could also be two completely new versions of a service. Different aspects can be measured spanning from runtime performance to implicit and

---

[1] http://goo.gl/8r9X3P.

© Springer International Publishing Switzerland 2016
I. Crnkovic and E. Troubitsyna (Eds.): SERENE 2016, LNCS 9823, pp. 133–148, 2016.
DOI: 10.1007/978-3-319-45892-2_10

explicit user behaviors. The results of those tests, as well as possibly some survey data (collected by prompting users to fill questionnaires evaluating their interaction with the website), are collected. Afterwards statistical tests are conducted to evaluate the existence of statistically significant differences between the two variants, thus leading to the acceptance or rejection of the null hypothesis, i.e. that there is no significant difference between the two versions [9]. A key issue is that the users should have a consistent experience for the service: they should always see the same variant when coming back to the service.

Although the efficacy and the value of A/B testing are testified by several years of use in multiple sites, it is mostly devoted to evaluate the usability aspects of a website [1] In light of evaluating A/B testing and its effect on e-commerce sales process, we identified the following research questions:

RQ1: *How can the use of A/B testing be extended from visual aspects of online services in order to optimize sales processes in the E-commerce domain?*
RQ2: *Can the aforementioned use of A/B testing be generalized to produce a framework that can be exploited by companies to create virtual assistants?*

To provide an answer to these questions we developed the Decision Assistant tool (`DA tool`) together with the company Sonician AB. `DA tool` provides to business owners the instruments to develop their own virtual assistants. This allows business owners to gain knowledge on their customer needs and to provide them with the product that fits them. To do this they can use the tool to create a step-wise process, which their customers have to follow. The steps composing the process are highly customizable, thus bearing the potential of creating several processes with different questions, number of steps and/or required information from the customer. This complex system offers an ideal base to conduct testing over the process itself, instead of conducting traditional user interface or usability tests, e.g., in terms of testing simpler processes against more complex ones.

The main conclusion of our work is that A/B testing is a promising technique for testing not only usability aspects (e.g. creating variations of the GUI of the site, such as different layouts, fonts, colours) but also aspects related to business processes. Thus, A/B testing might be exploited to enhance systems with a continuous verification and validation infrastructure allowing to experiment with the involvement of end users. Through such infrastructure the system itself can be able to experiment the parameters for triggering certain actions as a way to learn from large numbers of customers what the best response is.

The paper contributes also a list of lessons learned that should be taken into account to develop a framework to help companies creating their own virtual business assistants.

Paper structure: The remainder of this paper is structured as follows. Section 2 discusses related works in the field of controlled experiments in the web with particular focus on A/B testing approaches. Section 3 presents `DA tool` and its validation made by people working in Sonician AB. The performed experiments are presented in Sect. 4. Section 5 provides an answer to research questions and

Sect. 6 presents lessons learned. Section 7 provides concluding remarks and future work directions.

2   Related Works: Controlled Experiments in the Web

Although customer decision support systems are viewed as a promising selling tool, until recently, they had very limited application [4]. In the web 2.0 era, a system can offer a significant value to the entire sales process, guiding the customer to reach a buy-or-not decision [12]. Those systems find heavy use in the context of product configuration. Customer satisfaction can be determined in part by the easiness of the process the customer follows [5]. Another study shows that the customer is willing to pay more for a product when the effort to evaluate it took less, especially in cases where the customer is less skilled [3]. In general, the use of customer decision support systems can facilitate a solution driven approach to marketing [4].

Davenport expresses the importance of testing as a tool to make tactical decisions in a range of business settings, from banks to retailers to dot-coms, and stresses the need to create a testing mind-set in companies in order to move testing "*out of the laboratory and into the boardroom*" [2].

In online environments the goal of hosting controlled experiments is to perform the evaluation of new ideas in order to try and find out if those new ideas will grant any benefits compared to the previous arrangement of the system when applied [15]. As this is usually performed by companies or organizations, the ultimate benefit of conducting experiments is to increase return-on-investment [9]. This matter has been widely discussed in scientific literature, with the particularity that for web development this technique has been traditionally used to evaluate user experience aspects.

A/B testing has been widely used in web development as a kind of controlled experiment. When it comes to A/B testing, this has been applied to aspects concerning user experience or interaction with the website [7,8,15].

The idea of expanding A/B testing in online services from its initial (and somehow) traditional perspective of user experience has also been recently proposed by Hynninen and Kauppinen [6]. They conclude saying that A/B testing is a promising method in customer value evaluation. In this paper we provide a confirmation that A/B testing is a valid instrument to support the evaluation of E-commerce sales processes. Specifically, our aim is to prove its suitability not only in testing for webservice front-ends but also on evaluating sales process, specifically in the Business-to-Business (B2B) or Business-to-Consumer (B2C) perspective of automated sales.

A/B testing requires a large number of users involved in the experimentation [8,9]. This is especially true when dealing with variances that may be experienced by only a small share of the website users. It might actually be difficult to implement the testing infrastructure, since the experiments might involve an unusually large collection of data which must be managed in a reliable way. DA tool provides the testing infrastructure together with mechanisms to instantiate it to the specific needs of a certain company.

3   Decision Assistant Tool

DA tool has been conceived by closely working with a company focused in marketing automation in order to elicit the needed requirements for the development. This company is Sonician[2], which was originally established in 2008 as Sonician UK Limited, and from 2013 the main company is Swedish Sonician AB. The company is fully focused on marketing automation and helps other companies to get up and running using all aspects of marketing automation, i.e. Lead Capturing, Nurturing and Scoring.

DA tool has two types of users, the tool administrators and the end-users. The tool administrator is the business owner that wants to sell a product or a service; he is responsible for creating a flow of steps, called a Decision Assistant Flow or simply DA Flow. The end-user can either be a business or a private person, and his goal is to go through the Decision Assistant Flow in order to get information about a product or service. With the help of the DA tool an end-user comes to a decision on whether this product or service fits his needs.

3.1   Decision Assistant Flow

A DA Flow can provide information to the users through a wide array of items, such as images, videos, HTML formatted text, and diverse types of questions. DA tool supports the following types of questions:

Open questions - they do not have any predefined answer, instead the user inputs his text to describe either a problem or a situation or in general to provide feedback.

Single choice questions - the user must choose only one answer among a set of predefined answers.

Multiple choice questions - these questions are presented in a similar way as single choice ones, but with the particularity that the user is allowed to choose more than one answer.

The purpose of the flow can be to help the visitor of the website (i.e. the end-user) to ascertain whether the proposed product or service is exactly what he is looking for, or in its simplest use, to just inform the visitor about the product or service. The administrator of the flow can also assign a weight to each possible answer.

Once the visitor enters the flow and advances through it, the system keeps track of the selected answers, in order to conduct calculations with the weights. By the end of the flow the weight of each selected answer can be added up, and compared to a threshold value defined by the administrator in order to provide the visitor with either a positive or a negative suggestion.

Each step of the sales process can be represented within a Decision Assistant flow. It can either take an unaware visitor and inform him on the specific

---

[2] Sonician http://www.sonician.com/en.

product/service, or take a business contact and turn him into a client by successfully calculating his needs and suitability. The flow can start by making an introduction of the product or service, presenting some general information on its field of use and also the advantages that it can give to a potential owner. The visitors that decide to follow the flow can then be taken through a number of steps containing questions designed to assist him in order to gain any kind of information he needs.

A demonstration of the product can follow, either through a video presentation or images and text. By the end of the flow the visitor can learn whether his answers indicate that he would gain from using the product/service or not and also be required to enter his personal information in order to continue, or get more personalized feedback by email. The flow can also contain an order form to eliminate the need of any redirections if the visitor is about to make a purchase. It can be also utilized to represent the next steps of support and feedback as it can save the visitor ID for his later visits. Moreover, DA tool is engineered to enable future extensions, like for example a live chat tool to better facilitate the support step.

3.2   DA Tool Architecture

DA tool was designed using the Model-View-Controller (MVC) architecture. The Model part of the architecture includes a database module that contains all the building blocks needed to create DA tool. The database module is wrapped by another module that has the task of connecting the database tables to their model representations in the back-end of the tool. Any read/write operation on the database is going through that module. The Controller part of the architecture includes a module that is responsible for manipulating the models and passing the information to the graphical user interface. Also in the Controller there is a module responsible for handling the A/B tests, and one responsible for rendering the Decision Assistant flows. The View part of the architecture includes the two variations of the graphical user interface: the administrator side (flow editing tool) and the end-user side (flow display tool). The bulk of the development is made using the open source Laravel PHP framework (Controller). MySQL is used for the database (Model) and HTML5 along with jQuery, CSS3 and Bootstrap are used for the front-end of the web application (View). Also a lot of minor open source JavaScript libraries are used mostly for cosmetic reasons on the front-end side of the web application.

3.3   A/B Testing Capabilities of the Tool

The Decision Assistant tool offers A/B testing capabilities for the sales process part of the flow. It can range from variant sequence of questions and/or steps to status aids for the visitors. When the administrator is ready with the design of his Decision Assistant flow he has the option of cloning the whole flow and modifying this clone in order to produce the second variant (Treatment variant).

After choosing from one or more of the above possible modifications the newly created clone will be connected to the hash url of Control variant. Whenever there is a new visitor, one of the two variants of the flow is presented to them randomly with 50 % probability. Recurring visitors will always get the same variant they were first assigned to (provided of course they allow cookies or use the same system and browser to view the flow website). The results of each variant can be then reviewed individually and be compared in order to define which of the two can be more successful (in terms of successful outcomes), and help guiding the administrator in the design tactics for his future Decision Assistant flows.

3.4   Validation of DA Tool

Having a validated and approved `DA tool` is of key importance for the success of this research. Our goal is to validate the capability or suitability of the tool to conduct sales processes and help both the seller (the provider of the goods or services) and the customer into better understanding his needs. The validation has been performed through semi-structured interviews conducted with selected people within the Sonician AB company.

The selection of the appropriate subjects to be involved in the evaluation was decided in a meeting with our contact within the company, who, proposed a few candidates based on their role and suitability. This selection was further expanded during a general meeting of the company in which the authors presented the developed software. After this presentation, a brainstorming session was hosted in which participants were asked to provide ideas and target groups for the experiments. One of the managers offered himself to act as a contact person or "gatekeeper" [14] during the interviewing process, ensuring that all participants were informed and coordinating the different schedules and interviews. The selected subjects are shown in Table 1.

Table 1. Interviewees and their role in the company

Interviewee	Role
Number 1 (N1)	CEO & founder
Number 2 (N2)	Managing Director
Number 3 (N3)	Chief of Operations
Number 4 (N4)	Delivery Manager
Number 5 (N5)	Company Partner
Number 6 (N6)	Company Advisor
Number 7 (N7)	Company Advisor

In order to collect data, semi-structured interviews were conducted with all the participants. The purpose of the interviews was to validate `DA tool` and to assess whether it could be of help to the company. Interviews were also exploited to gain insight on factors that are important for creating online sales processes and Decision Assistant Flows. This will be particularly important for answering RQ2, as discussed in Sects. 5 and 6.

The interviews were conducted in accordance to guidelines proposed by Runeson and Höst [13]. Every session started with a semi-structured approach with very few questions predetermined. The semi-structured protocol strengthens the exploratory nature of the study. The structure of the interview might be found in [11]. Every session started with a semi-structured approach with seven predetermined questions. According to the answers on those questions the discussion was expanded to gather more feedback. Following recommendations in [13], and after asking for permission to each individual interviewee, each session was recorded in an audio format, since even though one of the interviewers was focusing on taking notes, it is hard to keep on all details. The interviews lasted about 25 min on average, with the longest lasting 45 min and the shortest 15 min.

Summarizing, the validation shows that DA tool received high praises from the company personnel and partners. Something highlighted in their responses was their certainty that DA tool could help them achieving their goals in marketing automation. Most of them had either heard of or had some experience with the tool before the interviews and thus they could actually verify that they tried and achieved what they wanted to do. A successful online process is, according to most of the interviewees, a process that is able to transmit to the customer a believable profit or benefit when the customer is looking for a product or a service. It must show this benefit in a clear way so that the purchasing decision is done without doubts by the customer. In turn, from the seller's perspective, a successful process is one that leads to a comparatively good number of conversions (purchases, acceptances). A successful process also must be tailored to the needs of each customer or customer group. The interviewees recognized that DA tool can support these beliefs through its' customization features and its' adaptability to any kind of sales environment.

4   Experiments

In order to provide an answer to the research questions RQ1 and RQ2 presented in the introduction we created two Decision Assistant flows in two different business domains. In the two experiments the AD flow creators created a flow using DA tool; more precisely, through the tool they defined a control and a treatment variant. The differences in those variants were based on the thoughts and ideas collected during the interviews described in Sect. 3.4.

According to Kohavi [9], the tests were carried out anonymously. This means that the subjects of the experiments did not know that they were being part of an online experiment. As part of the development of the tool, the authors created a script which acted as a load balancer; it distributed all participants randomly to one of the variants.

Once the participants entered the flow, there were two possible outcomes: finish the flow or drop-out at some point. Since the criteria to consider an experiment successful was for the participant to finish it, special care was taken in order to track the participant's status regarding completion of the flow. To achieve this, the tool would provide continuous tracking information to the authors, stating how many different participants started the flow and their status (seen, doing, or finished). In case of the 'doing' status, there might be two different possibilities: (i) the participant has stopped completing it but intends to resume it later, or (ii) the participant decided to drop out and will not complete the flow.

We also prepared a very short survey intended to obtain further feedback from the subjects (the target group) of the experiment. The survey was sent to each experiment participant approximately two to three weeks after the first send out. The reason was to get some insight on the cause for their completion or dropout of the flow, and suggestions on how to improve the process and the tool. Details about the survey might be found in [11].

First experiment - The first experiment was created by the first two authors of the paper also to test the tool and its functionalities. The purpose of the experiment was for testing the suitability of a future product that they are currently developing.

Characteristics of the variants: Both variants of the flow consisted of 5 steps, one of which was a "finishing/thank you" step. For the Control variant the questions were asked in a formal manner, and only relevant information was inquired. In the Treatment variant the questions were formed more relaxed using also a bit of humour. Some questions were added to each step that were focused on gathering more private information. With those two variants of the flow the authors want to see the differences between using a formal language or a more casual one but with the addition of more intrusive questions. This was for testing one hypothesis of one interviewed that asking for irrelevant question or for personal information would affect the behaviour of the interviewees. Another hypothesis we tested is that using language variations tailored to the target population might help.

Target group: The experiment involved 166 people, with age of the participants spanning from 18 to 35. Participants comes from different backgrounds, country of origin, and socio-economic environments.

Time span: The experiment started on 10th of September and ended on 18th of September, with the link of the flow posted in a social network.

Second experiment - This experiment was created by interviewee Number 7. The purpose of the experiment was to help the interviewee's company calculate its' client base's suitability for their product. Since the target group was completely comprised by Swedish speakers the flows were created in Swedish in order to facilitate their interaction with the flow.

Characteristics of the variants: The control variant consisted of 9 steps one of which was a "finishing/thank you" step. The first two steps had one question each while the rest consisted of 3 to 5 questions. Each answer had a specified weight with the end calculations leading to either a high suitability (success) or low suitability (failure). The visitors could get information about their status in the flow by a bar on the top of the screen, which showed the percentage of the flow that was completed at their current step. The treatment variant was made by merging some of the steps together resulting to a flow with 4 question steps. That way the visitors that were exposed to the treatment variant would see a bigger completion progress whenever they moved to a new step.

Target group: The experiment involved 141 persons from the client-base of the company.

Time span: The experiment started on Thursday 10th of September with the send-out of the link to the target group. The experiment was deemed finished at Friday 18th of September.

4.1   Results

Each experiment was examined individually through statistical analysis with the objective of reaching an understanding in whether there is a significant difference in the conversions among both the treatment and the control groups. In order to conduct this analysis, and since the values obtained from the experiments are categorical, the starting points are the contingency tables created during the analysis of the experiments. These contingency tables present the figures for both outcomes of the experiment, success or fail, and the variant to which they belong. Afterwards, a Pearson's Chi Squared test for fitness is conducted, in order to test whether there is statistical significance between the control and the treatment groups. Pure fails refers to participants who finished the flow and obtained a fail outcome, not accounting those participants who dropped-out. However, since the test is carried out using categorical variables, and the authors are only testing success and fail, dropouts will be added to those pure fails in the contingency tables created to account for total fails. The contingency tables show absolute numbers, which refer to actual participants tested on each group, and not percentages, even though for better understanding of the reader, we also use percentages to describe each experiment's result. Regarding whether the Yates's correction should be applied or not to a Chi-squared test, the decision is not to apply it, given the fact that both the sample size and the cell count are large enough (cell count refers to the figure in each cell) in the experiments, and also it tends to give very conservative p-values.

First experiment -   This experiment, as explained above, was created by the first two authors. A target audience of mostly young people, aged 18–35, was selected for this experiment. While most of those participants are based in Europe, some of them are based in North and South America as well as Africa. Also, some of those based in Europe have origins in other regions, and this adds for a more diverse sample. The tracking tool included in the Decision Assistant showed that, out of the 166 participants, 91 and 75 participants were respectively redirected to Variant A and Variant B. The conversion goal set for this experiment was to achieve as many successful complete interactions as possible. The created flow was configured in the Decision Assistant using weights to measure the answers provided by the subjects of the experiment. Upon completion of the flow, and based on the calculations of the final score with the weights of the answers selected, the subject was tested either as successful or failed. Regarding the 91 participants that conducted Variant A, 79 % of them finished the flow and 21 % dropped out during the process. `DA tool` shows that 65 % of the test were successful, and 14 % failed. Combining pure fails and dropouts, a total of 35 % of participants are hence considered as fail (see Fig. 1). Extrapolating the data to focus only on the results for finished flows, a total of 82 % of those were successful, while only 18 % were tested as failed. Regarding Variant B, 75 % of the 75 subjects who participated finished the flow, while 25 % of them dropped-out. Over the total figures, a 68 % of the sample tested as successful, while a comparatively low 7 % tested as pure failed. The combined pure fails and drop-outs make the total failures rising to a 32 % (see Fig. 1). Focusing on only-finished cases, a quite high 90 % of the participants who finished tested positive, leaving a 10 % as failed.

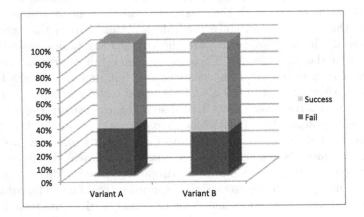

Fig. 1. Experiment 1

Variant A was presented with a formal language, and it boasted a lower rate of drop-outs. However, even though Variant B presented a more vulgar language, the fact that the target was predominantly a young audience helped to keep both comparatively high finish and conversion rates. Another characteristic of Variant B was to ask for more private questions such as personal information on economic stability, with the idea of getting an insight on whether this would make participants wary or suspicious about giving this kind of information. Of those who finished Variant A with successful results, eight participants refused

Table 2. First experiment: contingency table

	Non converted (Fail)	Converted (Success)
Variant A	32	59
Variant B	24	51

to give their personal information, while for Variant B with positive results, all of them provided the personal information requested. More discussion about this can be found in Sect. 5. The corresponding contingency table for this experiment might be found in Table 2.

The test was performed using an online tool called Graphpad[3]. The resulting figures show a sufficiently large sample size and cell count, resulting in a $\chi^2 = 0.184$ and a p-value of p = 0.3339 with one degree of freedom. Thus the null hypothesis is accepted and the result for this test is that there is no significant difference between the two groups.

Second experiment - As described above, this experiment targets real customers of a company. DA `tool` showed that out of the 142 subjects, 78 and 64 of them were taken to Variant A and Variant B, respectively. As specified in the description of the experiment Variant B had fewer steps with comparatively more questions each than Variant A. DA `tool` shows that for Variant A 23 % of the participants completed the flow, having a high rate of success. Thus, as shown in Fig. 2, in total, 77 % of the subjects dropped-out at the beginning or during the process. 22 % of those that ended the process are successes and only 1 % result as pure fails. Combined, the total number of failures sums up 78 % of participants. Focusing on those that completed the process, 95 % of them successfully completed and 5 % failed completing, although this figures are not accounted for the statistical test performed.

Variant B shows a lower 11 % of finished processes out of the total size, however with a 100 % success rate among those, and consequently no rejections in this partial analysis. In total, this variant makes up for an 11 % of conversions, with a total of 89 % of participants achieving a fail status (see Fig. 2).

Regardless of the apparent success of Variant B over finished processes, the analysis is based on the total data, including those who did not finish the flow as failed. Then, data show a big difference among variants, indicating that shorter steps adequately classified and separated might make up for a more dynamic interaction with the system, and thus encouraging participants to stay and complete the process. With these values, the contingency table for the second experiment is shown in Table 3.

In appearance, variant A shows a higher rate of conversions with a comparatively close sample size. However, statistical analysis will show whether there is an actual difference between variants. Having plotted the figures obtained from the experiment, a Chi-squared test was performed. The null hypothesis presented

---

[3] http://graphpad.com/quickcalcs/contingency1/.

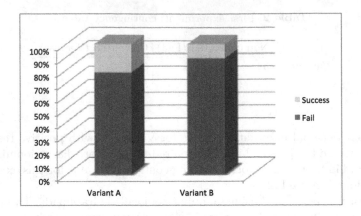

Fig. 2. Experiment 2

Table 3. Second experiment: contingency table

	Non converted (Fail)	Converted (Success)
Variant A	61	17
Variant B	57	7

was that there is no significant difference between the two groups. The test was performed using, as for the first experiment, the Graphpad tool. The resulting one-tailed p-value of this test is p = 0.0429 and $\chi^2 = 2.951$, which is lower than 0.05. Therefore, we can reject the null hypothesis, and it can be considered that there is a significant difference among control and treatment variances, with Variant A obtaining a better conversion rate.

4.2 Threats to Validity

For what concerns construction validity, as the research aims to provide conclusions based on quantitative data, the need for a sufficient sample size is essential. In our experiments we have a good number of people participating to the experiment and the experiments are conducted over real samples. Also to reduce bias during the selection of subjects for the interviews a "gatekeeper" at the company was used.

Another potential threat can be found on internal validity. Internal validity refers to the risk of interference in causal relations within the research. Since the first part of the study has been performed cooperating with seven employees of the company, there is a threat of them manipulating the variants of the web sites so that the experiment will throw the results they personally aim for, instead of real business objectives. The first two authors of the paper revised and supervised the experiment 2 and the third author supervised the experiment 1 in order to reduce this threat to validity.

One potential threat can also be found with regards to the external validity and specifically to what extend can the findings be generalized in order to produce a suitable answer for the second research question. This is alleviated by the fact that the company in which the experiments took place cooperates with other companies which would allow the experiments to have a much more wider target group than just that of a single company.

Finally, Kohavi [10] points out that while carrying split tests it is possible to know which variant is better, but not the reason why it is better. This limitation can be solved by additionally collecting users' comments. This study addresses this limitation by providing a short questionnaire to the experimental subjects, in order to complement the experiments.

5   Discussion

In this section we provide an answer to the research questions RQ1 and RQ2 by considering the answers from the interviews and the results of the experiments. *RQ1: How can the use of A/B testing be extended from visual aspects of online services in order to optimize sales processes in the E-commerce domain?* The results of the interviews showed a promising perspective into integrating this type of split testing in the E-commerce domain. All sources agreed on the suitability of DA tool in order to create online sales processes, and they all provided a good insight on what they believe a successful online sales process must offer to the end customer. Among them, the most cited are to provide a believable benefit, an easy to use system, a relation with the customer based on trust in the form of being transparent about your process, and having a good strategy. The second experiment shows a significant difference between the two tested variants. Variant A obtains a better conversion rate, as corroborated by the statistical analysis of the data gathered. This gives the authors the idea that shorter steps encourage people to engage in completing the process in a successful way.

To sum up, A/B testing is a promising instrument for the optimization of sales processes; more experiments might be needed to understand advantages and limitations of using A/B testing in this domain.

RQ2: Can the aforementioned use of A/B testing be generalized to produce a framework that can be exploited by companies in the field to create virtual assistants? Based on the conducted study, A/B testing is a promising way to test out improvements when conducting online sales processes. The most cited characteristic to create a successful online sales process was to avoid using irrelevant questions. The irrelevancy of the questions might put users in fear of the real intentions of the owner of the process, such as the intention of acquiring unnecessary data from the users, be it personal data or directly useless information.

This request for useless information might also give the user the impression of a poor strategy from the business side, or even worse, the fact that the business is incapable of communicating the features of a product or the details of a service. From the experimentation it could also be inferred that steps featuring a short number of questions tend to lead to more conversions than hosting a process with fewer, more dense steps. It is worth, nonetheless, to test more extensively this characteristic in order to obtain a better understanding of its benefit in different settings.

Another characteristic that arose from the interviews is the possibility of reordering questions, since it was stated that it is often difficult to come up with a good logical order for them in the beginning. Testing with variants hosting the same questions but organized in different patterns or paths can help to solve this situation. Moreover, the possibility of having different paths for the user adds for more variety in the treatments, which further expands the possibilities of A/B Testing.

Summarizing, the study made in this paper represents a first step towards the creation of a framework that can be used by business owners to create virtual assistants to exploit A/B testing for checking e-commerce sales processes.

6   Lessons Learned

This section reports lessons learned from (i) our collaboration with Sonician AB, (ii) the performed interviews, (iii) the two experiments, and (iv) feedbacks received from the participants to the experiments.

Having a good Strategy: Before initiating the online sales process a factor that could lead to its success is the strategy of the seller. The plan of action must be decided beforehand.

Need of Trust: Being able to achieve a certain level of trust with the website visitor is also something required for a successful online sales process.

Size matters and Easy next step: The second experiment testifies that the size of the flow should be as small as possible. Having a too long process might cause a user to drop out. This effect can be made worse by combining long processes with irrelevant questions or not giving the user feedback on his progress. Ease of use during the sales process is also a very important factor. The visitor must be able to easily find his way through the order forms and product/service information so that he can take the next step without much confusion.

Creating Believable Benefit: A believable benefit would mean that the visitor of the website can get something either for free or for a bargain price by buying the product that is offered. This believable benefit could also be tailored for each specific visitor. Another issue that was noted was that the flow does not feature an *I don't know* answer. This reinforces the belief that when making a flow that helps the customer identify his needs, it should be taken into consideration that not all customers are aware of everything that surrounds the product. Providing answers such as *I don't know* could help figuring out the customer's level of knowledge on the subject, which in turn can help the decision assistant in providing better results.

Capture Leads: Just as the lead capturing system can lead the visitor to the information he wants it is equally important that this information exists and is of a certain standard that is easily understandable and relevant. Feedbacks received on the first experiment highlight that the major reason to dropout the experiment is related to a lack of interest from the participants. This means that in order to improve the response ratio in a decision assistant flow a lot of consideration must be placed in the format in which it will be presented to potential customers.

Professional website and proper language: A professional looking website is obviously of the utmost important for a successful online sale. A professional looking website can never exist without showing user testimonies and references from well known persons or organizations that use the service that is on sale. The main issue with communication is to know who is the target audience, with the objective of using an appropriate language.

7   Conclusion and Future Work

In this paper we investigated and experimented the use of A/B testing out of the traditional visual aspects. Our study shown that there are positive indications on the suitability of A/B testing experiments that focus on sales processes. Interviews conducted with the Sonician AB personnel concluded that, using DA tool developed specifically for this purpose, A/B testing could be an interesting instrument for evaluating sales processes.

As future work it would be valuable to perform further experiments to better assess the suitability and the limitations of A/B testing into a domain which is different from visual aspects, and especially into E-commerce environments. The authors suggest experimentation to be carried into a wide variety of target groups, including B2B and B2C environments.

References

1. Bosch, J.: Building products as innovation experiment systems. In: Cusumano, M.A., Iyer, B., Venkatraman, N. (eds.) ICSOB 2012. LNBIP, vol. 114, pp. 27–39. Springer, Heidelberg (2012)
2. Davenport, T.H.: How to design smart business experiments. Harvard Bus. Rev. **87**(2), 68–76 (2009)
3. Garbarino, E.C., Edell, J.A.: Cognitive effort, affect, and choice. J. Consum. Res. **24**(2), 147–158 (1997)
4. Grenci, R.T., Todd, P.A.: Solutions-driven marketing. Commun. ACM **45**(3), 64–71 (2002)
5. Huffman, C., Kahn, B.E.: Variety for sale: Mass customization or mass confusion? J. Retail. **74**(4), 491–513 (1998)
6. Hynninen, P., Kauppinen, M.A.: B testing: a promising tool for customer value evaluation. In: Proceedings of RET 2014, pp. 16–17, August 2014
7. Kaufmann, E., Cappé, O., Garivier, A.: On the complexity of A/B testing. In: Proceedings of the Conference on Learning Theory, Junuary 2014

8. Kohavi, R., Deng, A., Frasca, B., Longbotham, R., Walker, T., Xu, Y.: Trustworthy online controlled experiments: Five puzzling outcomes explained. In: Proceedings of KDD 2012, pp. 786–794. ACM, New York, NY, USA (2012)

9. Kohavi, R., Henne, R.M., Sommerfield, D.: Practical guide to controlled experiments on the web: listen to your customers not to the hippo. In: Proceedings of KDD 2007, pp. 959–967. ACM, New York, NY, USA (2007)

10. Kohavi, R., Longbotham, R., Sommerfield, D., Henne, R.: Controlled experiments on the web: survey and practical guide. Data Min. Knowl. Discovery 18(1), 140–181 (2009)

11. Koukouvis, K., Alcañiz Cubero, R.: Towards extending A/B Testing in E-Commerce sales processes. Master thesis, Chalmers University of Technology, Department of Computer Science and Engineering, Gothenburg, Sweden (2015)

12. O'Keefe, R.M., McEachern, T.: Web-based customer decision support systems. Commun. ACM 41(3), 71–78 (1998)

13. Runeson, P., Höst, M.: Guidelines for conducting and reporting case study research in software engineering. Empirical Softw. Eng. 14(2), 131–164 (2009)

14. Shenton, A.K., Hayter, S.: Strategies for gaining access to organisations and informants in qualitative studies. Educ. Inf. 22(3–4), 223–231 (2004)

15. Young, S.W.H.: Experience, improving library user with A, B testing: principles and process. Weave J. Libr. User Experience 1(1), (2014). doi:12535642.0001.101

Author Index

Printed in the United States
By Bookmasters